Ron

Travel Guide 2024

Embark on an Epic Journey Through Romanian Culture, Unravel Its Intriguing History, and Create Unforgettable Experiences

Rose Bordelon

Romania

DISCLAIMER & COPYRIGHT NOTE

This travel guide is protected by copyright law. Reproduction, distribution, or transmission in any form without the author's prior written permission is prohibited, except for brief quotations in critical reviews and certain noncommercial uses allowed by copyright law. Unauthorized reproduction or distribution may result in civil and criminal penalties, including fines and imprisonment. Readers have a limited license for personal, non-commercial use; any other use requires explicit written permission. By accessing and using this guide, readers agree to respect the outlined copyright and disclaimer provisions.

The information in this guide is based on the author's experiences, research, and knowledge up to the publication date. While efforts have been made to ensure accuracy, the author and publisher are not liable for changes, inaccuracies, or omissions after this date. Travel conditions may change, and readers should independently verify details before

Romania

making arrangements. The author and publisher do not assume responsibility for readers' actions following the guide, as travel involves inherent risks. Readers are advised to exercise caution and make informed decisions based on their individual circumstances.

Copyright © 2024 Rose Bordelon

Romania

Prologue

Romania is a mysteriously beautiful and utterly charming country located in the center of Eastern Europe, where folktales from antiquity coexist with contemporary energy. Shut your eyes and allow me to transport you through its alluring scenery and rich history.

Imagine yourself meandering through Transylvania's cobblestone alleyways, where medieval castles rise out of mist-covered slopes like specters. Perched atop precipitous bluffs, the fabled Bran Castle watches over this area, its turrets penetrating the heavens akin to the spires of a medieval castle. Within its walls, the murmurs of centuries-old mysteries blend with the echoes of Dracula's legacy, luring visitors into a realm where myth and reality collide.

However, Romania is far more alluring than only its famous castles. Explore the interior of the Carpathian Mountains, where pristine

Romania

woods conceal secret valleys and pure streams wind through unspoiled terrain. Here, the sound of songbirds fills the air, and the land holds amazing and uncommon riches. Nestled between these rocky peaks is the enigmatic area of Maramureş, where old traditions still flourish and time appears to have stopped in charming towns with elaborately carved wooden churches.

The rich plains of Transylvania and the undulating hills of Bukovina, where fields of vivid wildflowers spread as far as the eye can see, are revealed as you travel southward like a living tapestry. Time-honored traditions still exist here in the heart of rural Romania, from vibrant folk festivals honoring marriages and harvests to the eerie sounds of traditional music resonating through town squares.

But the kindness and hospitality of Romanians may be its greatest asset. Take in the rich fabric of Romanian culture, where every area has its

Romania

own distinct traditions, folklore, and culinary combinations. Savor the rich fragrances of freshly brewed coffee in bustling city cafés, indulge in substantial feasts of sarmale and mămăligă, or immerse yourself in the rhythmic swirl of traditional dances performed under starry sky.

Are you prepared to go out on a journey that will never be forgotten, my darling traveler? As you explore Romania's rich fabric of history, culture, and scenic beauty, let me be your guide. There are countless delights waiting to be found in this region of magic, from the sun-kissed coasts of the Black Sea to the gloomy depths of ancient woods.

Romania

Monasteries

Romania

Castles

Romania

Sibiu

Romania

Brasov

Romania

Table Of Contents

Introduction _____ **10**
Chapter 1: Getting to Know Romania _____ **16**
   Quick Fun facts about Romania _____ 16
   Overview of Romania's Geography and Climate 19
   Brief History and Cultural Background of Romania _____ 23
   Practical Information _____ 27
Chapter 2: Planning Your Trip _____ **32**
   Seasons/Weather _____ 32
   Best Time to Visit Romania _____ 34
   Transportation Options _____ 36
   Accommodation Options _____ 40
   Budgeting and Cost Considerations _____ 51
Chapter 3: Bucharest: The Capital City _____ **57**
   Exploring Bucharest's Iconic Landmarks _____ 57
   Museums, Galleries, and Cultural Attractions in Bucharest _____ 61
   Dining and Nightlife Options _____ 65
Chapter 4: Transylvania: Land of Legends ___ **71**
   Exploring the Medieval Charm of Brasov, Sibiu, and Cluj-Napoca _____ 71
   Exploring Dracula's Castle and Other Historic Sites _____ 75
   Outdoor Adventures in the Carpathian Mountains _____ 78
Chapter 5: The Painted Monasteries of Bucovina _____ **83**

Visiting UNESCO World Heritage-Listed
Monasteries with Stunning Frescoes _____ 83

Exploring the Traditional Villages and
Landscapes of Northern Romania _____ 87

Chapter 6: The Danube Delta: Europe's Amazon 92

Exploring the Tranquil Waterways of the
Danube Delta: A Guide to Cruising and
Kayaking _____ 92

Birdwatching and Wildlife Spotting
Opportunities _____ 96

Traditional Fishing Villages and Local Cuisine __ 101

Chapter 7: Maramures: Timeless Traditions _ 107

Experiencing the Rural Charm and Wooden
Churches of Maramures _____ 107

Witnessing Traditional Festivals and
Celebrations _____ 111

Homestays and Cultural Enthralment
Experiences _____ 116

Chapter 8: Black Sea Coast: Sun, Sand, and Sea 122

Relaxing on the Beaches of Mamaia and
Constanța _____ 122

Water Sports and Recreational Activities in
Mamaia and Constanța _____ 126

Exploring Ancient Ruins and Seaside Resorts _ 132

Chapter 9: Romanian Cuisine and Culinary Experiences _____ 138

Introduction to Romanian Cuisine and Regional
Specialties _____ 138

Romania

Food Tours, Cooking Classes, and Culinary Experiences_____ 146
Chapter 10: Travel Tips and Resources_____152
Safety Tips_____ 152
Money-Saving Tips_____ 156
Health and Medical Information_____ 158
Useful Phrases in Romanian_____ 161
Chapter 11: Itinerary Suggestions_____ 169
Outdoor Adventure Itinerary: Exploring the Natural Wonders of Romania_____ 169
Cultural Enthralment Itinerary: Discovering Romania's Rich Heritage_____ 174
Family-Friendly Itinerary: Fun and Adventure for All Ages_____ 178
Conclusion_____ 183
Appendix_____ 185
Maps of Romania and its major Cities_____ 185
Travel Guides by Rose Bordelon_____ 193

Romania

Introduction

In the heart of Eastern Europe lies a land of timeless beauty and enduring mystery - Romania. From the misty peaks of the Carpathian Mountains to the sun-drenched shores of the Black Sea, this enchanting country beckons travelers with its rich tapestry of history, culture, and natural wonders. But to truly understand Romania, one must delve into its storied past, where legends intertwine with reality to create a captivating tale of resilience and triumph.

Our journey through Romania begins centuries ago, amidst the ruins of ancient Dacia, a land

Romania

inhabited by fierce warriors and skilled craftsmen. Here, amid the rugged terrain and dense forests, the seeds of Romanian identity were sown, as tribes united under the banner of King Decebalus to resist the might of the Roman Empire. For years, they fought valiantly against overwhelming odds, their defiance immortalized in the rocky cliffs of the Orăștie Mountains, where Decebalus' face was carved into the stone as a testament to their indomitable spirit.

But it was not until the dawn of the medieval era that Romania truly began to flourish, as the kingdoms of Wallachia, Moldavia, and Transylvania emerged as bastions of culture and civilization in the heart of Europe. Under the rule of legendary figures such as Vlad the Impaler and Stephen the Great, Romania's borders expanded, its cities thrived, and its people forged a legacy that would endure for generations to come.

Romania

Yet, amidst the triumphs of the past, Romania has also known moments of great adversity. In the tumultuous years of the 20th century, the country faced invasion, occupation, and the brutal repression of totalitarian regimes. But through it all, the Romanian people remained steadfast in their determination to preserve their identity and their freedom, their resilience a testament to the strength of the human spirit.

One such moment, etched indelibly in the annals of Romanian history, is the Revolution of 1989. As the Iron Curtain began to crumble across Eastern Europe, the people of Romania rose up against the oppressive regime of Nicolae Ceaușescu, demanding an end to tyranny and a return to democracy. What began as a series of protests in the streets of Timișoara soon spread across the country, culminating in a dramatic showdown in the heart of Bucharest's Revolution Square. In the

Romania

face of gunfire and repression, the Romanian people stood united, their courage and sacrifice paving the way for a new era of freedom and democracy.

Today, as Romania embraces its place on the world stage, the echoes of its past resonate in every corner of the country, from the medieval castles of Transylvania to the vibrant cities of Bucharest and Cluj-Napoca. Join me as we embark on a journey through the pages of history, exploring the hidden wonders and unforgettable moments that have shaped the destiny of this extraordinary land. Welcome to the Travel Guide to Romania - where the past comes alive, and adventure awaits around every corner.

Chapter 1: Getting to Know Romania

Quick Fun facts about Romania

Here are some amazing Romanian facts:

1. **Legendary Dracula:** Romania is frequently associated with Bram Stoker's Dracula mythology. Dubbed "Dracula's Castle," Bran Castle in Transylvania draws hordes of curious tourists drawn by the legend.

Romania

2. **Diverse Terrain:** Romania is home to the second-largest delta in Europe, the Danube Delta, undulating hills, rich plains, and the Carpathian Mountains.

3. **Ancient Dacia:** The Dacians, who were known for their expert warriors, lived in the ancient territory of Dacia, which is located in modern-day Romania. Later, after the Roman conquest in the second century AD, it became a province.

4. **Literary Enthusiasm:** Romanians read a lot, which is a sign of their rich literary heritage. Numerous bookstores, libraries, and literary events are held across the nation, including the yearly National Book Day, which is observed on April 23.

5. **Creative Minds:** Throughout history, Romania has produced a large number of innovators and inventors. Nicolae Paulescu invented insulin, Henri Coandă invented the jet

Romania

engine, and Petrache Poenaru invented the fountain pen.

6. **Bright Folklore:** Legends, traditions, and supernatural creatures abound in Romanian folklore. Similar to vampires, strigoi is a well-known myth. Romania's traditional clothes, music, and dances add significant cultural elements to the nation.

7. **Palatial Marvel:** With more than 1,000 rooms, the Palace of the Parliament in Bucharest is the largest administrative edifice in the world and the heaviest structure on Earth. Built during the dictatorship of Nicolae Ceaușescu, it is a masterpiece of architecture.

8. **Animal Sanctuary:** The Carpathian Mountains provide vital habitat for a variety of animals, including brown bears, wolves, lynx, and wild boars, which are all found in Romania. Romania is therefore one of the last remaining wild places in Europe.

Romania

---

9. **Culinary Treasures:** The delicious blend of Turkish, Hungarian, and Austrian flavors is Romanian food. Taste buds are enticed by specialties like mămăligă (cornmeal porridge), mic (grilled sausages), and sarmale (cabbage rolls).

10. **Majestic Castles:** Romania is home to several magnificent castles and fortifications, including Peleș Castle, Corvin Castle, and Rasnov Citadel, all of which are rich in architectural beauty and rich in history, in addition to Bran Castle.

These fascinating facts offer an insight into the fascinating history, culture, and natural beauties of Romania.

Romania

Overview of Romania's Geography and Climate

Romania is a country in Southeast Europe with a varied terrain that includes beautiful mountains and verdant plains, all shaped by the country's moderate continental climate. Here's a detailed rundown:

Geographical:

1. **Carpathian Mountains:** The Carpathians, which include a large portion of central and northern Romania, are a magnificent arc that provides beautiful scenery and opportunities for outdoor activities. At 2,544 meters, the tallest mountain, Moldoveanu, draws hikers, climbers, and lovers of the outdoors.

2. **Transylvania:** Transylvania, which makes up a large portion of central and northwest Romania, is well-known for its legendary charm, medieval cities, and fortified cathedrals.

Romania

Its magnificent scenery, which includes rolling hills, woods, and old castles, draws tourists from all over the world.

3. **Dobrogea:** Dobrogea, a region of extremes in southeast Romania, is home to the verdant Danube Delta, a UNESCO World Heritage Site brimming with animals, and the dry Dobrogea Plateau, renowned for its unusual rock formations and historic monuments.

4. **Danube River:** The second-longest river in Europe and an essential waterway for commerce and transit, the Danube River borders Romania on the south. Its bountiful floodplains sustain farming while serving as homes for a wide variety of plants and animals.

5. **Black Sea Coast:** The Black Sea meets Romania's eastern border; it is home to lively coastal cities like Constanta and Mamaia, as well as sandy beaches and resorts. Sun-seekers

Romania

go to the Black Sea's warm waters throughout the summer.

Weather:

Romania's diversified terrain contributes to its varying climate:

1. **Temperate-Continental Climate:** This climate, which is prevalent across most of Romania, has marked seasonal variations with hot summers and frigid winters. In the lowlands, summertime temperatures may rise, while wintertime brings frost and snow.

2. **Mountain Climate:** The Carpathian Mountains get more snowfall and cooler temperatures, especially at higher altitudes. Because of the moderate summers, it's a great place to go skiing and trekking in the winter.

3. **Mild Coastal Climate:** Compared to interior regions, Romania's climate is milder along the Black Sea coast, with warmer winters

Romania

and cooler summers. This makes it a well-liked location for lovers of water sports and beachgoers.

4. **Transitional Climate:** A few areas, such as Dobrogea, have a climate that is in between continental and marine influences. In comparison to inland locations, summers are warmer and winters are milder.

All things considered, Romania's varied topography and climate have something to offer any kind of visitor, whether it is leisure on sand beaches along the Black Sea coast, cultural discovery in ancient cities, or outdoor experiences in the highlands.

Brief History and Cultural Background of Romania

Historical Foundations: The history of Romania spans thousands of years, with evidence of human habitation dating back to

Romania

the Paleolithic period. Numerous tribes and civilizations have inhabited the region, most notably the Dacians who did so before the Roman conquest in the first century AD.

Roman Influence: Dacia and Moesia Inferior, two territories of the Roman Empire that later included Romania, are the origin of the country's name. The construction of cities, roadways, and fortifications as well as the spread of Christianity are among the long-lasting effects of the Romans.

Medieval Period: Roman, Byzantine, Slavic, and Hungarian civilizations were among those that shaped Romania throughout this time. Major medieval states with distinct cultures, languages, and rulers, such as Moldavia, Wallachia, and Transylvania, emerged in the region.

Ottoman Rule and Independence: The Ottoman Empire annexed a large portion of

Romania

southeast Europe, including parts of Romania, in the fifteenth century. Wallachia and Moldavia, two Romanian kingdoms, were subjugated by the Ottoman Empire, although Transylvania continued to be ruled by Hungary. Nonetheless, a spirit of resistance to Ottoman rule persisted, leading to Romania's eventual independence in the 19th century.

Unity and Modernization: Wallachia, Moldavia, and Transylvania, three Romanian principalities, were united into a single nation-state in the 19th century. Significant modernization efforts were also carried out during this period, such as the abolition of serfdom, the establishment of a constitutional monarchy, and the growth of infrastructure and industry.

Communist Era and World Wars: Romania had instability throughout the 20th century, taking part in both World Wars I and II. Romania was ruled by Nicolae Ceaușescu, a

Romania

communist, from 1965 to 1989, after World War II. Repression, hardship on the economic front, and political exclusion characterized this period.

Transition to Democracy: The fall of communism in 1989 was a watershed in Romanian history and ushered in a phase of democracy and market economic development. Romania became a member of the Euro-Atlantic group when it joined the European Union in 2007 and NATO in 2004.

Romania's rich and varied cultural heritage is a reflection of its lengthy history of being influenced by many different civilizations and ethnic groups. Roman, Byzantine, Ottoman, and Western European ancestry are all represented in Romanian traditions, folklore, music, dance, cuisine, and architecture.

Romania is home to a diverse population that makes up the country's cultural mosaic,

Romania

comprising Romanians, Hungarians, Roma, Germans, Ukrainians, and other ethnic groups. The languages, religions, cultures, and traditions all reflect this diversity.

A rich tapestry of influences spanning millennia and encompassing various civilizations defines Romania's history and cultural heritage. Romania has progressed from its historical beginnings to its current era of democracy and inclusiveness while retaining its traditions and identity.

Practical Information

Visa Requirements: For the majority of visitors, Romania offers a visa-free program for brief stays of up to 90 days throughout 180 days to citizens of the EU, EEA, and several other nations, such as the US, Canada, Australia, and Japan. It is important to confirm the necessary visa requirements before traveling, since regulations may vary based on

Romania

one's nationality and intended duration of stay. Obtaining a visa could be essential for extended stays or specific goals like employment or study.

Money: The Romanian Leu (RON) is the country's official currency. For the best prices, it is recommended to convert currencies at banks or approved exchange bureaus. Major cities and tourist destinations usually accept credit and debit cards, but it's always a good idea to bring additional cash, especially if you're heading to a smaller town or rural location where card acceptance may be limited.

Language: Romanian, a Romance language closely related to Italian, French, Spanish, and Portuguese, is the official language of Romania. Although Romanian is the primary language spoken across the country, English is also widely spoken, especially among young people and in tourist areas, hotels, and restaurants. You could run upon Hungarian or German

Romania

speakers in areas with sizable populations of either language.

Transportation: Domestic airlines, trains, buses, and an ever-expanding road network are all part of Romania's well-developed transportation system. Buses and railroads connect major cities including Timisoara, Brasov, Cluj-Napoca, and Bucharest, providing rapid and affordable travel options. In cities, taxis are widely available, however, it's advisable to use authorized taxis and settle on the fare in advance.

Health and Safety: Romania generally maintains high standards for healthcare, with major cities having easy access to hospitals and other medical services. Getting travel insurance that pays for medical costs—including emergency evacuation—is advised. While bottled water is readily available and often used, tap water is usually safe to drink in urban areas. It's important to take the standard

Romania

precautions to ensure personal safety while traveling, as with any destination. These include being aware of your surroundings and avoiding isolated areas at night.

Electricity: 50Hz frequency and 230V standard voltage are used in Romania. Type F power outlets accept plugs with two round pins as well. It could be necessary for visitors from nations with different plug types to bring a plug adapter to use their electrical devices.

Romanian customs and manners are unique in terms of culture and manners. A handshake is customary while extending greetings, and acceptable eye contact is expected throughout conversations. It's important to dress modestly and politely, covering your knees and shoulders, when you attend places of worship. Tipping is customarily appreciated in dining establishments, taxis, and other services; the standard gratuity is around 10% of the whole cost.

Romania

By being acquainted with these useful components, you can ensure a seamless and relaxing journey when visiting Romania. Whether visiting historic cities, hiking in the Carpathian Mountains, or relaxing on the Black Sea coast, Romania offers a wide range of activities and attractions for visitors of all stripes.

Romania

Chapter 2: Planning Your Trip

Seasons/Weather

Romania offers a variety of seasons, each with its personality and allure. The best time to go will depend on your tastes and areas of interest. An outline of the seasons and what to anticipate is provided here:

Spring (March to May)
As the weather begins to warm up and the countryside comes alive with vibrant blooms, spring is a wonderful time of year to visit

Romania

Romania. With comfortable temperatures between around 10°C and 20°C (50°F and 68°F), it's a great time of year for outdoor pursuits like cycling, hiking, and seeing historic towns without the summertime crowds.

Summer (June to August)

Because of the pleasant weather and longer daylight hours, summer is Romania's busiest travel season. Higher temperatures are possible, especially in July and August, when most localities have highs between 25°C and 30°C (77°F and 86°F). This is the ideal time of year for outdoor activities, beach vacations along the Black Sea, and going to festivals and events.

Autumn (September to November)

With the foliage changing to a kaleidoscope of red, orange, and gold hues, autumn is a beautiful time of year to visit Romania. The weather is still pleasant, with gradually lower temperatures from September through

Romania

November. Nature lovers could take advantage of this season to visit historic castles surrounded by autumnal colors, go wine tasting in Transylvania, or explore the Carpathian Mountains.

Winter (December to February)
Most of Romania experiences snow and cold temperatures during this season, especially in the mountainous regions. Winter sports fans are drawn to ski areas such as Poiana Brasov and Sinaia because of their picturesque surroundings and excellent snow conditions. Christmas markets and holiday festivities enhance the charm of the season in urban areas, while Transylvania's castles and fortified churches look breathtaking when covered with snow.

Best Time to Visit Romania

The best time to visit Romania will depend on your hobbies and interests. Fall and spring

Romania

provide the best weather and fewer crowds for outdoor activities and tourism. Winter is fantastic for skiing, winter sports, and taking in Romania's festive spirit; summer is great for beach vacations and exploring the countryside. However, The summer months of June through August are the best and busiest to travel to Romania. It's scorching outside and doesn't rain very often. During this time, daytime highs should be around 30°C (86°F). Though it's only apparent in places where tourism is the primary attraction, like Brasov or Sibiu, these are the busiest months of the year for travel. Even still, compared to Western Europe, the crowds are far less.

Visits during the shoulder seasons (late April to May and September to October) are also highly recommended. For anyone planning to go hiking in the hills, you'll have much milder temps and avoid the throng. Although there is more rain in the spring, the autumn offers breathtaking foliage that provides a

Romania

picturesque backdrop for your journey, particularly if you are visiting Transylvania. Romanian winters can be extremely frigid, with temperatures well below zero. Snowfall is frequent but not abundant, which may have an impact on driving conditions. Because of the influence of Soviet architecture and its reliance on flat, gray concrete, Bucharest has a considerably grimmer vibe in the winter than places like Sighișoara and Brașov. To put it briefly, unless you have a special desire to experience the quiet and frigid cities, I wouldn't suggest going there in the winter.

Romania is a fascinating year-round destination with a wealth of cultural heritage, breathtaking landscapes, and kind hospitality, regardless of the season.

Transportation Options

Romania offers a variety of transportation options to satisfy the needs of every visitor,

Romania

whether they are visiting the vibrant city, breathtaking countryside, or small rural towns. An overview of the different transit options is provided below:

Flights

Henri Coandă International Airport (OTP) in Bucharest is the largest of the international airports serving Romania. Iași International Airport (IAS), Timișoara Traian Vuia International Airport (TSR), and Cluj-Napoca International Airport (CLJ) are further noteworthy airports. Domestic flights provide a quick and effective way to travel long distances inside the country, connecting important cities like Timișoara, Cluj-Napoca, Iași, and Bucharest.

Trains

Traveling between towns and regions is made convenient and affordable by Romania's wide railway network. The majority of rail services are operated by Căile Ferate Române (CFR), a

Romania

state-owned company that has lines that go from east to west and from north to south throughout the country. There are trains for every budget and timetable, ranging from faster, more advanced InterCity services to slower regional trains. The main railway hub is Bucharest, which has frequent trains to locations all around Romania.

Buses

In Romania, buses are a popular mode of transportation, especially for destinations that are not served by airports or trains. Numerous private bus operators provide luxury coaches with amenities like Wi-Fi and air conditioning on intercity and international trips. Major towns and villages have bus stops, which provide access to both urban and rural areas. Local and international bus services are centered at Autogara Filaret, Bucharest's main bus terminal.

Car Rentals

Romania

If you want the flexibility to explore Romania at your own pace, renting a car is a great option. Large vehicle rental companies have facilities in airports, train stations, and city centers. They provide a wide selection of automobiles to suit different preferences and price ranges. Romania has an extensive and well-maintained road network, which facilitates easy driving between cities and tourist destinations. But especially in rural areas, drivers need to be aware of potential hazards, road conditions, and local traffic laws.

Local transit

To get about in cities and towns, people may rely on options like buses, trams, and trolleybuses. While neighboring cities like Cluj-Napoca, Timișoara, and Iași have efficient public transportation systems, Bucharest has an expansive metro system. In cities, taxi services are also readily available; nevertheless, it is advisable to use authorized taxis and settle on the fare in advance of the journey.

Romania

Romania offers easy and accessible travel options for visitors to see its stunning landscapes, vibrant cities, and rich cultural past thanks to its many transportation options. Romania offers travel options for all types of enthusiasts, including scenic train journeys, road trips to unexplored gems, and intercity flights.

Accommodation Options

Romania provides a broad selection of lodging alternatives to meet any traveler's interests and budget, from opulent hotels to comfortable guesthouses and budget-friendly hostels. Here's a summary of the numerous kinds of housing available:

Hotels

Romania provides a choice of hotels ranging from high-luxury properties to budget-friendly alternatives. Major cities like Bucharest,

Romania

Cluj-Napoca, and Brasov have a broad range of multinational hotel chains, boutique hotels, and family-run facilities. Hotels in Romania often provide pleasant rooms, contemporary amenities, and services such as on-site restaurants, bars, fitness centers, and conference facilities. Many hotels additionally give free breakfast and Wi-Fi for guests.

Here are a few of them:

1. **Grand Hotel Continental (Bucharest):** Located in Bucharest's Old Town, the five-star Grand Hotel Continental is housed in a historic building that dates back to 1886. Personalized concierge services, a gourmet restaurant serving fine dining, a modern bar, and lounge, a wellness center with spa treatments, and elegant rooms and suites decorated with antique furniture and plush fabrics are all features of the hotel.

Property Features

Romania

Parking, Free High-Speed Internet (WiFi), Hot tub, Fitness Center with Gym / Workout Room, Bar/Lounge, Bicycle rental, Airport transportation, Business Center with Internet Access.

Room features

Air conditioning, Room service, Safe, Minibar, Flatscreen TV.

Room types

Non-smoking rooms, Suites, and Family rooms.

Location: Calea Victoriei 56, Bucharest 010083 Romania.

2. **Hilton Sibiu (Sibiu):** Located in the charming Transylvanian city of Sibiu, the Hilton Sibiu offers tasteful accommodations encircled by the magnificent Carpathian Mountains. Large guest rooms and suites with modern conveniences, a rooftop terrace with

Romania

panoramic views, an indoor pool, a fitness facility, many dining options, and flexible event spaces for corporate events and weddings are all features of the hotel.

Property Features

Parking, Free High-Speed Internet (WiFi), Pool, Fitness Center with Gym / Workout Room, Bar/Lounge, Skiing, Airport transportation, Business Center with Internet Access.

Room features

Air conditioning, Private balcony, Room service, Safe, Minibar, Flatscreen TV.

Room types

Non-smoking rooms, Suites, and Family rooms.

Location: Strada Padurea Dumbrava 1, Sibiu 550399 Romania.

Romania

3. Aurelius Împăratul Romanilor:

Constructed in 2006, the hotel complex is located at an elevation of 1030 meters along the beaches of Miorita Lake in the Poiana Brasov resort. It exudes the elegance and grandeur of the Tirol Alps, and the towering structure provides a singular panorama of the Postavaru Mountain's ski slope. The opulent tourism complex has meeting spaces, private secured parking, a restaurant with a terrace overlooking the lake, and a hotel, all of which are flawlessly blended into the surrounding natural environment.

Property Features

Free parking, Free High-Speed Internet (WiFi), Pool, Fitness Center with Gym / Workout Room, Free breakfast, Skiing, Billiards, and Business Center with Internet Access.

Room features

Romania

Bathrobes, Room service, Safe, Bottled water, Minibar, Flatscreen TV, Extra long beds, Bath/shower.

Room types

Non-smoking rooms, Suites, Family rooms, and Smoking rooms are available.

Location: Poiana lui Neagoe 25, Poiana Brasov 500001 România.

Guesthouses (Pensiuni)

For a more genuine and personal experience, try staying at a traditional guesthouse or "pensiune" in Romania. These family-run lodgings are frequently situated in attractive rural locations, historic towns, or lovely pastoral settings. Guesthouses provide pleasant accommodations with rustic décor, home-cooked meals highlighting local delicacies, and individual hospitality from the hosts. Guests may enjoy activities like hiking,

Romania

horseback riding, and cultural excursions offered by the guesthouse owners.

Pensiuni-based guesthouses:

1. **Casa Mica (Sighișoara):** Situated in the old citadel of Sighisoara, Casa Mica is a lovely guesthouse housed in a 17th-century historic building. The guesthouse offers individually tailored hospitality from the owners who provide local knowledge and suggestions for touring the area, as well as quaint rooms with classic style and a courtyard garden with outdoor seating. A cooked breakfast is given every day.
Location: 76 Strada General Petre Popovat, Bucharest.

2. **Pensiunea Belmonte (Bran):** This family-run guest house is surrounded by stunning Transylvanian scenery and is located close to Bran Castle. The guesthouse offers large, rustically designed rooms and suites, a

Romania

typical Romanian restaurant with homemade food, a wine cellar filled with regional wines, and outdoor pursuits like hiking, horseback riding, and guided cultural tours.
Location: Complex Turistic, Sambata de Sus 505200 România.

3. **Pensiunea Casa Cartianu (Sinaia):** Located in the resort town of Sinaia, against the backdrop of the Bucegi Mountains, this property offers quaint accommodations in a tranquil setting. The guesthouse has well-furnished rooms with views of the mountains, a garden patio with grilling facilities, a common kitchen and dining area, and personalized service from the hosts, who can arrange transportation and outdoor activities.
Location: DJ 664 282, Târgu Jiu 217531, Romania.

Hostels

Romania

Budget-conscious tourists may choose hostels, which offer economical lodging in shared dormitory rooms or individual rooms. Hostels are prominent in large cities and tourist locations, providing basic facilities such as community kitchens, common spaces, free Wi-Fi, and social events. Hostels are a popular alternative among backpackers, independent travelers, and young people wishing to meet other travelers and experience Romania on a budget.

Here are a few hostel suggestions:

1. **Transylvania Hostel (Cluj-Napoca):** This hostel offers reasonably priced rooms in a prime position and is situated in the vibrant city of Cluj-Napoca. The hostel offers both private rooms and common kitchen and lounge areas, free WiFi, organized social events and activities, and helpful staff who can recommend nearby restaurants and activities.

Romania

2. **Kismet Dao Hostel (Brașov):** This charming hostel with traditional Romanian architecture is located in Brașov's historic center. The hostel offers communal kitchen and dining space, free tea and coffee, private rooms and bunk beds, a garden terrace with views of the mountains, a common lounge with a fireplace, and a friendly atmosphere ideal for meeting other travelers.

3. **The Shelter Hostel in Bucharest:** Conveniently situated next to University Square, The Shelter Hostel offers affordable accommodation. The hostel has private and dorm rooms, a fully equipped kitchen for self-catering, free Wi-Fi, a common area with a TV and board games, and helpful staff who can help with travel plans and sightseeing tours.

These examples demonstrate the wide range of accommodation options available in Romania that suit different traveler preferences, interests, and price ranges. Whether you like

Romania

opulent hotels, cozy guesthouses, or affordable hostels, Romania has the right accommodations to make your trip more enjoyable.

Rural Homestays: For a genuinely immersive cultural experience, consider staying at a rural homestay or "agrotourism" accommodation in Romania's countryside. These lodgings give the chance to stay with local families, enjoy traditional Romanian hospitality, and engage in agricultural activities like harvesting, cheese production, and wine tasting. Rural homestays give comfortable lodgings, home-cooked meals served with fresh, local products, and the ability to interact with nature and the local community.

Alternative lodging: In addition to hotels, guesthouses, and hostels, tourists may also discover alternative lodging alternatives in Romania, such as vacation rentals, bed and breakfasts, campgrounds, and eco-lodges.

Romania

These alternatives appeal to varied tastes and interests, whether you're seeking a private hideaway in nature, a pleasant urban apartment, or a unique cultural experience.

With its varied choice of hotel options, Romania provides something for every tourist, whether you're seeking luxury and comfort, rustic charm, or budget-friendly accommodations. By picking the best lodging for your requirements and interests, you may improve your trip experience and create memorable memories in Romania.

Budgeting and Cost Considerations

Traveling in Romania might be reasonably reasonable compared to other European countries, but it's vital to budget properly to get the most out of your vacation. Here are some budgeting strategies and cost considerations to help you plan your expenses:

Romania

Accommodation

- **Budget:** Hostels and guesthouses provide economical alternatives for budget-conscious tourists, with dormitory beds beginning at roughly €10-€20 per night. Private rooms in guesthouses or inexpensive hotels normally vary from €20-€50 per night.
- **Mid-range:** For mid-range lodgings, plan to spend between €50-€100 per night for a nice hotel room or bed and breakfast.
- **Luxury:** Luxury hotels and resorts in Romania may vary from €100-€300 or more per night, depending on the location, facilities, and season.

Transportation

- **Flights:** Domestic flights inside Romania are quite reasonable, with rates beginning at roughly €30-€100 for

Romania

one-way tickets, depending on the route and prior booking.

- **Trains:** Train travel is a cost-effective way to see Romania, with rates beginning at roughly €5-€20 for shorter excursions and €20-€50 for longer routes in second class.
- **Buses:** Bus tickets are often cheaper than trains, with rates beginning at roughly €5-€15 for shorter trips and €15-€30 for larger ones.
- **Car Rentals:** Renting a car may be reasonably reasonable, with daily prices beginning at roughly €20-€50 for a small car, minus gasoline and insurance charges.

Food & Dining

- **Street Food:** Street food sellers provide good and reasonable snacks and meals, such as "mici" (grilled sausages), "covrigi" (pretzels), and pastries, beginning at roughly €1-€5 per item.

Romania

- **Local Restaurants:** Dining at local restaurants and cafés is budget-friendly, with pricing for typical Romanian meals ranging from €5-€15 per meal. A three-course dinner at a mid-range restaurant may cost between €15-€30 per person.
- **Supermarkets:** Shopping in supermarkets and grocery shops is a cost-effective method to save money on meals and snacks, with costs for goods and basics similar to other European nations.

Activities and Attractions

- **Free Attractions:** Numerous churches, squares, and historic sites—among Romania's cultural icons—offer free admission or a nominal fee.
- **Guided Tours:** Depending on the duration, destination, and activities

Romania

covered, guided tours and excursions may incur additional costs.

- **Outdoor Activities:** Depending on the activities you choose and the cost of renting equipment, taking in Romania's natural attractions, like hiking in the Carpathian Mountains or visiting the Danube Delta, may be affordable or completely free.

Other Costs:

- **Tipping:** Although not required, tipping is valued in Romania. Tipping between 5 and 10% is customary at restaurants, cafés, and cabs for exceptional service.
- **Mementos:** Set aside money for gifts and mementos, such as locally made clothing, handicrafts, and textiles. The cost of these goods will depend on their rarity and quality.
- **Miscellaneous:** Establish a contingency fund to provide peace of

Romania

mind when planning for unanticipated expenses like emergencies, entry fees, and delayed transportation.

You may have a pleasant and affordable holiday in Romania while taking in its stunning landscapes, vibrant cities, and rich cultural past by carefully planning and budgeting for lodging, transportation, food, activities, and incidentals.

Romania

Chapter 3: Bucharest: The Capital City

Exploring Bucharest's Iconic Landmarks

Romania's vibrant capital, Bucharest, is a historical, cultural, and architectural treasure trove. Explore the many historical sites, which include the majestic Palace of Parliament and the charming Old Town alleys.

Here's a look at some of the most recognizable sites in Bucharest:

Romania

1. **Palace of Parliament (Palatul Parlamentului):** The Palace of Parliament is a stunning feat of architecture and design that honors Romania's socialist past. It's breathtaking to see, being the second-largest administrative building in the world. Entering its opulent halls, adorned with marble floors, crystal chandeliers, and gorgeous furnishings, is an utterly captivating experience. Don't pass up the chance to take a guided tour to discover more about the building's fascinating past and be in awe of its astounding size.

You cannot help but feel the weight of history bearing down on you as you stand in the vast halls of the Palace of Parliament. The building's grandeur is bemusing, yet its beauty and craftsmanship are obvious. You may get insight into Romania's history and the perseverance of its people by exploring its maze-like corridors and listening to tales of its construction.

2. **Old Town (Lipscani):** Take a stroll around Bucharest's Old Town, where vibrant

Romania

architecture, quaint cafés, and lively taverns bring history to life. This historic area has a diverse range of architectural styles, including art nouveau façades, opulent houses, and ancient churches. Enjoy the atmosphere by taking a leisurely stroll, stopping for a traditional meal or coffee at one of the neighborhood eateries, and taking in the odd assortment of shops and boutiques that sell anything from handcrafted goods to vintage finds.

Wandering about Bucharest's Old Town is like taking a trip back in time. There's a lot of energy and excitement in the bustling squares, hidden courtyards, and narrow lanes. Every turn offers a fresh discovery and an insight into the city's rich cultural legacy, whether you're perusing antique shops or enjoying a cup of coffee at a sidewalk café.

3. **Revolution Square (Piața Revoluției):** Show your admiration for the recent history of Romania by visiting the site of the 1989

Romania

uprising that resulted in the fall of communism. Notable locations include the Memorial of Rebirth, which honors the revolutionaries, and the former Royal Palace, which is now the National Museum of Art. Give the events that transpired here and the bravery of those who fought for freedom and democracy some thought.

Being in the middle of Revolution Square, surrounded by historic structures and monuments, makes one feel somber and reflective. The serene but melancholic atmosphere serves as a reminder to guests of the people of Romania and the sacrifices they made to achieve their independence. It serves as a reminder that history should be valued and respected in addition to being something to be remembered.

Discovering the major places of Bucharest is an enthralling journey through the history and culture of Romania, where new facets of its culture, history, and natural beauty are

Romania

revealed at every turn. You will get enmeshed in the rich tapestry of Bucharest's history whether you are admiring the magnificence of the Palace of Parliament, meandering through the Old Town's narrow streets, or paying tribute to the revolutionaries.

Museums, Galleries, and Cultural Attractions in Bucharest

Romania's vibrant capital, Bucharest, is home to several museums, art galleries, and cultural venues that showcase the rich history, customs, and art of the nation. Discovering top-notch art collections and captivating exhibits on Romanian culture and traditions awaits all art enthusiasts. Culture aficionados in Bucharest should not miss these must-see locations:

1. **National Museum of Art of Romania (Muzeul Național de Artă al României):** The National Museum of Art of Romania is the premier art institution in the nation, and it is

Romania

located in the former Royal Palace on Revolution Square. Its vast collection includes ornamental arts, holy relics, paintings, sculptures, and other works of art from centuries of European and Romanian artists. Highlights include masterpieces by European artists including Rembrandt, Rubens, and El Greco, as well as pieces by well-known Romanian painters like Nicolae Grigorescu and Theodor Aman.

2. **Romanian National Peasant Museum (Muzeul Național al Țăranului Român):** Nestled in a stunning neo-Romanian building in Victory Square, the Museum of the Romanian Peasant is a cultural gem dedicated to preserving and commemorating ancient Romanian art and practices. With exhibits on rural life, traditional crafts, costumes, pottery, and religious symbols, this distinctive collection provides insight into the rural customs and traditions of the nation. The lively folk art market inside the museum is a

Romania

must-see, offering unique handicrafts and mementos for sale.

3. **Village Museum (Muzeul Național al Satului "Dimitrie Gusti"):** This outdoor ethnographic museum in Herastrau Park allows visitors to go back in time and experience rural Romanian history. The museum, which spans 30 acres, has more than 300 painstakingly restored medieval houses, churches, windmills, and workshops from different parts of Romania that highlight rural architecture and culture. Wander around the charming rural settings, see artisan demonstrations, and discover the traditions and customs of Romania's many ethnic groups.

4. **Theodor Pallady Museum (Muzeul Theodor Pallady):** Honoring the life and contributions of one of Romania's most significant modern artists, the Theodor Pallady Museum is housed in a charming house in the Cotroceni neighborhood. Pallady's paintings,

Romania

drawings, and personal belongings are on display in full at the museum, providing insight into his creative process and sources of inspiration. In addition to seeing Pallady's vivid still lifes, landscapes, and portraits, visitors may take in temporary exhibitions that include pieces by other Romanian artists.

5. **Cotroceni Palace and National Museum (Palatul Cotroceni și Muzeul Național Cotroceni):** The Romanian president's official residence, Cotroceni Palace and National Museum (Palatul Cotroceni și Muzeul Național Cotroceni) offers visitors an opportunity to explore its opulent interiors and fascinating past. The palace's spectacular rooms, which include the presidential office, reception halls, and private quarters and are furnished with exquisite furnishings, original artwork, and historical artifacts, may be explored with guided tours. Through pictures, documents, and relics, the museum's exhibits delve into Romania's political and cultural past,

providing a window into the nation's development throughout the decades.

Experience the wealth of Bucharest's cultural heritage by going to its galleries, museums, and other cultural institutions; each visit will take you on an illuminating and educational journey. You may explore Romania's history, discover its rural cultures, or enjoy works of art, among many other opportunities to extend your perspective and deepen your appreciation for this intriguing country.

Dining and Nightlife Options

Bucharest has a vibrant dining and nightlife scene, with a wide range of eateries, cafés, bars, and clubs to suit every preference. The city's culinary and entertainment offerings are sure to please even the most discerning visitor, offering everything from traditional Romanian food to international cuisines and inventive drinks. Here's a quick look at some of

Romania

Bucharest's best options for dining and entertainment at night:

Dining:

1. **Caru' cu Bere:** Housed in a beautifully restored historic building, Caru' cu Bere is one of Bucharest's most famous restaurants. Step back in time here. This well-known restaurant serves traditional Romanian food to patrons in a lively setting with folk performances and live music. Savor delicacies like grilled sausages, packed cabbage rolls, and fried doughnuts with jam and sour cream, known as "papanasi."
Opening hours: 9 am -12 am Everyday
Location: Strada Stavropoleos 5, București 030081, Romania.

2. **Hanul lui Manuc:** Located in the center of Bucharest's Old Town, Hanul lui Manuc offers the charm of a traditional Romanian inn. This old establishment, which dates back to the early 19th century, serves hearty Romanian food in a rustic environment with exposed

Romania

brick walls and wooden beams. Sample dishes include "mamaliga" (polenta), "mititei" (grilled minced pig buns), and "ciorba de burta" (tripe soup).

Opening hours: 10 am -12 am Everyday
Location: Str. Franceză 62-64, București 030106, Romania.

3. **Locanta Jaristea:** This chic restaurant, renowned for its creative cuisine and stunning design, serves premium Romanian cuisine with a modern twist. This trendy restaurant, which is close to Revolution Square, serves elegant cuisine made with seasonal produce and inventive takes on classic Romanian fare. For a really unique dining experience, pair your meal with a selection of Romanian wines or house-made cocktails.

Opening hours: 11 am -11 pm every day, Saturday 24-hours
Location: Strada George Georgescu 50-52, București 040133, Romania.

Romania

Nightlife:

1. **Old Town (Lipscani):** With a multitude of bars, pubs, and clubs along its cobblestone alleyways, Bucharest's Old Town is a hive of nightlife. There is something for everyone to enjoy, from modern cocktail lounges and lively nightclubs to charming wine bars and craft beer pubs. Wander around the bustling squares and alleys, have a glass of wine at a rooftop bar, or spend the evening dancing to DJ sets and live music.

2. **Control Club:** Bucharest's top underground music venue and nightclub, Control Club is situated in a former industrial neighborhood in the city center. This alternative hotspot attracts a diverse crowd of music enthusiasts with its extensive lineup of live bands, DJs, and electronic performers. Take in a live performance in the small concert theater, lounge on the terrace, or dance to the newest sounds on the main floor.

Opening hours: 12 pm - 5 am every day

Romania

Location: Strada Constantin Mille 4, București 010142, Romania.

3. **Fratelli Social Club:** Visit Fratelli Social Club, a stunning club and bar in Herastrau Park, to get a taste of Bucharest's affluent nightlife. Reputable for its sophisticated ambiance, exuberant parties, and celebrity encounters, Fratelli is a preferred location for the city's social elite. Savor premium drinks, get VIP bottle service, and listen to top DJs spin the newest tunes until the wee hours of the morning.

Location: Strada Glodeni 1-3, București 077190, Romania

Bucharest offers a wide range of dining and nightlife options to suit every mood and occasion, whether you want to savor regional Romanian food, sample cuisines from across the world, or dance the night away in a chic nightclub. Take in the vibrant energy of the city as well as the delicious food and exciting

Romania

entertainment options that make Bucharest a popular travel destination for people from all over the world.

Romania

Chapter 4: Transylvania: Land of Legends

Exploring the Medieval Charm of Brasov, Sibiu, and Cluj-Napoca

With its centuries-old architecture, fortified walls, and winding cobblestone lanes, Romania's medieval cities are like pages from a fairy tale. Discovering Brasov, Sibiu, and Cluj-Napoca is like taking a time travel to a realm inhabited by merchants, craftsmen, and

Romania

knights. A glimpse of these beautiful towns' medieval splendor is shown here:

1. **Brasov:** This charming city surrounded by the Carpathian Mountains is tucked away in the center of Transylvania. Discover the wonders of its remarkably untouched medieval town, which includes the famous Black Church, Council Square, and one of Europe's tiniest alleys, Strada Sforii (Rope Street). See the old St. Nicholas Church, stroll the defensive walls at your leisure for sweeping views of the city, and don't miss the impressive Brasov Citadel perched on Mount Tampa.

The cable car ride to the peak of Mount Tampa offers breathtaking views of Brasov and the surrounding area. There's nothing quite like being on top of the hill and looking down upon Brasov's medieval roofs—it transports you to another realm.

2. **Sibiu:** Formerly known as Hermannstadt, Sibiu is a charming city in the center of

[Romania](#)

Transylvania that is renowned for its vibrant cultural scene and well-preserved medieval architecture. Discover the UNESCO World Heritage Site, the old center, with its cobblestone streets, pastel-colored houses, and ornate churches. The famous Brukenthal Palace, the Bridge of Lies, and the Evangelical Lutheran Cathedral, with its magnificent Gothic architecture, are among the highlights. Explore the squares and alleyways of Lower Town; you'll find artisan workshops, peaceful cafés, and hidden courtyards.

Discovering the ancient passageways and staircases of Lower Town is similar to diving into a labyrinth of secrets that remain to be solved. From hidden courtyards to quaint artisan shops, every corner offers a new revelation that reveals more about Sibiu's rich past and cultural legacy.

3. **Cluj-Napoca:** Cluj-Napoca, the unofficial capital of Transylvania, is a vibrant metropolis with an intriguing blend of modern and

Romania

medieval architecture. Discover the historic Old Town, which combines contemporary cafés, hip stores, and art galleries with a beautiful blend of Gothic churches, Baroque palaces, and medieval squares. Explore Union Square, pay a visit to the imposing St. Michael's Church, and take in the stunning Matthias Corvinus House. Don't pass up the chance to explore Cluj-Napoca's historic citadel ruins, which provide expansive views over the city and the surrounding area.

From Austro-Hungarian homes to medieval fortifications, Cluj-Napoca's Old Town offers a diverse range of architectural designs and cultural influences for visitors to explore. There's a story waiting to be discovered around every corner, so visitors of all ages can go on an exciting journey of discovery.

Discovering the medieval splendor of Brasov, Sibiu, and Cluj-Napoca is an adventure through the rich cultural heritage and history of Romania, where each step reveals a new

Romania

aspect of the nation's fabled past. Beautiful cobblestone streets, bustling town squares, fortified walls, and majestic castles—these charming towns provide a glimpse into a bygone era that continues to attract tourists from all over the world.

Exploring Dracula's Castle and Other Historic Sites

Romania's ancient monuments, castles, and fabled landmarks bring the country's rich history and tradition to life. Bran Castle is one of the most well-known, sometimes linked to the famed Dracula tale. A sneak peek into seeing Dracula's Castle and other historical places in Romania is provided here:

1. **Bran Castle (Castelul Bran):** Because of its connection to the real Vlad the Impaler, Bran Castle, which is perched on a rocky hill amid the lovely Transylvanian landscape, is often associated with the Dracula legend. Even

Romania

while the castle itself only has a passing relationship to the Dracula legend, it's nonetheless an interesting place to visit. Explore the castle's rooms, hallways, and courtyards to discover its past as a royal mansion, a fortified military installation, and a museum honoring Queen Marie of Romania. There is a feeling of wonder and mystery as you climb the winding stairway to the castle's towers, which give expansive views of the surrounding area. Bran Castle is a once-in-a-lifetime experience, whether you want to explore the medieval rooms, take in the exquisite furnishings and relics, or just take in the ambiance of this iconic location.

2. **Peleş Castle (Castelul Peleş):** One of Romania's most magnificent royal homes, Peleş Castle is a Neo-Renaissance architectural masterpiece that lies tucked away in the picturesque Carpathian Mountains close to the town of Sinaia. Constructed for King Carol I in the late 1800s, Peleş Castle has sumptuous

Romania

interiors filled with priceless artwork, elaborate woodcarvings, and sumptuous furniture. Discover the opulent chambers of the castle, including the magnificent reception hall, royal chambers, and the magnificent armory museum, with an astounding assortment of armaments and armor.

Entering Peleș Castle's elaborate hallways is like entering a fairy tale, with each chamber narrating a narrative of splendor and wealth. The magnificent marble staircase and the exquisitely designed rooms envelop guests in an opulent and elegant realm of royalty.

3. **Sighișoara Citadel (Cetatea Sighișoara):** One of Romania's best-preserved walled cities, the medieval citadel of Sighișoara is situated in the center of Transylvania and is recognized as a UNESCO World Heritage Site. Discover the city's cobblestone walkways, vibrant homes, and historic structures, such as the recognizable Clock Tower, which provides sweeping city

Romania

views. Discover the origins of Vlad the Impaler, sometimes referred to as Dracula and the myths and history that surround this ancient treasure.

It seems as if you have traveled back in time to the Middle Ages while meandering through the Sighișoara Citadel's winding lanes and secret courtyards. For both history lovers and cultural vultures, the well-preserved architecture, lively market squares, and extensive history make it an enthralling trip.

Discovering Romania's rich history and mythology via visits to Dracula's Castle and other historical places is an intriguing experience. Every stop gives a window into Romania's illustrious history and the ongoing heritage of its renowned buildings, from the fabled halls of Bran Castle to the sumptuous chambers of Peleș Castle and the medieval alleyways of Sighișoara Citadel.

Romania

Outdoor Adventures in the Carpathian Mountains

The Carpathian Mountains provide an abundance of outdoor activities, distinct ecosystems, and stunning scenery, making them a haven for nature lovers. In this breathtaking natural paradise, there is something for everyone to enjoy, from hiking and mountain biking to wildlife observation and winter sports. Here's a preview of what the Carpathians have to offer in terms of outdoor experiences:

1. **Hiking & Trekking:** Take a foot tour of the Carpathian Mountains by tracing a system of well-signposted routes that wind through verdant forests, mountain meadows, and rugged peaks. There are routes suitable for every interest and ability level, from easy day hikes to strenuous multi-day excursions. The Retezat and Fagaras Mountains are well-liked hiking destinations where you may summit

Romania

Romania's highest peaks and take in breathtaking sweeping vistas.

2. **Wildlife Watching:** A wide range of plants and animals, like wolves, lynx, brown bears, and several bird species, may be found in the Carpathian Mountains. Set out on a local guide-led wildlife-watching tour to see these rare creatures in their natural habitat. See rare species like golden eagles and chamois by visiting national parks like Piatra Craiului and Bucegi.

3. **Mountain Biking:** Get on your saddle and go for the Carpathian Mountains on a mountain biking excursion. There is a variety of terrain to explore for both beginner and expert riders, from quiet forest routes to rugged singletracks and challenging descents. Discover undiscovered gems and breathtaking vantage points by renting a bike or taking a guided tour along the way.

Romania

4. **Skiing and Snowboarding:** The Carpathian Mountains become a snow-covered wonderland in the winter, offering excellent opportunities for skiing and snowboarding. Go to popular ski resorts including Poiana Brasov, Sinaia, and Predeal, where you can enjoy modern lifts, well-maintained slopes, and a range of amenities for lovers of winter sports. The Carpathians provide an abundance of chances for snow-filled adventures, whether you're cruising off-piste or doing turns on the pistes.

5. **Rock Climbing and Mountaineering:** The Carpathian Mountains provide thrilling opportunities for anyone looking for a vertical challenge. Try your skills on routes that range from beginner-friendly to expert-level, on granite crags, alpine peaks, and limestone cliffs. To learn the ropes and see some of the most well-known climbing locations in the area, sign up for a guided climbing trip or enroll in a mountaineering school.

Romania

6. Eco-Tourism and Cultural Experiences: Take part in eco-tourism activities that showcase regional cuisine, crafts, and customs to fully dive in the rich cultural history of the Carpathian Mountains. See remote settlements tucked away in the highlands, where you may interact with local artisans, indulge in handcrafted foods, and discover ancient traditions passed down through the ages.

There are many opportunities for outdoor exploration and discovery in the Carpathian Mountains, from heart-pounding adventures to serene nature retreats. Experience the excitement of the slopes, tranquility in the forest, or cultural enthralment in far-off towns—the Carpathians will leave you with a deep appreciation for Romania's breathtaking natural beauty and unforgettable memories.

Romania

Chapter 5: The Painted Monasteries of Bucovina

Visiting UNESCO World Heritage-Listed Monasteries with Stunning Frescoes

Numerous monasteries recognized for their elaborate construction, spiritual value, and beautiful paintings are located in Romania and are included as UNESCO World Heritage sites. Visitors from all over the globe are drawn to these historic sites because they provide a window into the nation's artistic and religious

Romania

traditions. This is a guide to seeing some of the most famous monasteries with breathtaking paintings in Romania:

The eight Orthodox monasteries that make up the Painted Monasteries of Bucovina are situated in the northeastern part of Romania and are well-known for their colorful murals that include biblical scenes, saints, and religious themes.

Voronet Monastery: known as the "Sistine Chapel of the East," is a highlight due to its elaborate murals from the 15th century and recognizable blue facade. Other noteworthy monasteries with distinctive architectural designs and creative masterpieces include Moldovita, Sucevita, and Humor.

Strolling about the courtyard of Voronet Monastery, with its imposing walls covered in vibrant murals, is a very engrossing experience. Visitors are taken to another era and location by the artwork's vivid colors and minute

Romania

details, which also provide a window into the rich cultural legacy of Bucovina's monastic traditions.

Monastery of Horezu: Located in southern Romania, the Monastery of Horezu is a UNESCO World Heritage Site and a masterwork of Brancoveanu-style architecture. Prince Constantin Brancoveanu founded the monastery in the 17th century, and it is well known for its elaborate internal decorations, carved stone façade, and beautiful murals. The church's walls and ceilings are covered with elaborate artwork that portrays scenes from the lives of saints and events from the New Testament.

Entering the Monastery of Horezu's courtyard, adorned with graceful arches and verdant gardens, transports one to the height of the Brancoveanu dynasty's glory. The monastery's beautiful architecture and calm ambiance make it a tranquil getaway from the busyness of everyday life.

Romania

Monastery of Sucevita: Situated in the Bukovina historic district, the Monastery of Sucevita is well-known for its remarkably intact 16th-century paintings. The monastery's outside walls are covered with ornate murals that portray scenes from the Apocalypse, the Life of Jesus Christ, and the Last Judgment, among other stories. Art and history lovers should make a trip to Sucevita because of the frescoes' rich detailing and vivid hues. Strolling around the outside walls of the Monastery of Sucevita, with its imposing defenses and vibrant murals, seems like traveling between spiritual and historical eras. Understanding the cultural and religious importance of this architectural jewel is made possible by the elaborate artwork and religious symbolism.

Exploring Romania's rich cultural and artistic legacy is made possible by visiting the monasteries that have been inscribed on the

Romania

UNESCO World legacy list, which are known for their breathtaking paintings. Each location offers an amazing voyage of discovery and enlightenment, whether one is enjoying the vivid paintings of Bucovina's Painted Monasteries, marveling at Horezu's architectural splendor, or exploring the religious meaning of Sucevita.

Exploring the Traditional Villages and Landscapes of Northern Romania

Snuggled among undulating hills, verdant woods, and picturesque valleys, traditional villages may be found in Northern Romania, an area rich in culture, history, and visual beauty. Set off on an adventure across this scenic area to uncover quaint towns, antiquated customs, and stunning scenery. Here's a guide to discovering northern Romania's traditional villages and landscapes:

Romania

1. **Maramures:** A region in northern Romania, Maramures is well-known for its traditional handicrafts, well-preserved wooden churches, and rustic way of life. Discover the villages of Breb, Sighetu Marmatiei, and Barsana, where residents uphold ancient customs and traditions and the streets are lined with wooden buildings with elaborately carved facades. Explore the wooden churches of Bârsana, Surdesti, and Plopis, which are designated by UNESCO and have ornate paintings and 17th-century architectural elements.

With horse-drawn carts, haystacks, and vibrant flower beds decorating the environment, strolling through the towns' winding alleyways will transport you to a fairytale setting. A look into a more straightforward way of life, where history and legacy are valued and conserved, may be found in Maramures' serene atmosphere and timeless beauty.

Romania

2. **Bucovina:** Located in northern Romania, Bucovina is well-known for its breathtaking scenery, traditional crafts, and painted monasteries. Discover the woodworking, weaving, and pottery traditions of the villages of Vama, Ciocanesti, and Marginea. Explore the colorful paintings that cover the outside walls of the UNESCO-listed Painted Monasteries of Voronet, Moldovita, and Sucevita. These murals include scenes from the Bible and the lives of saints.

The stunning scenery and enduring charm of the region's communities will enthrall you as you drive through its verdant farmland and rolling hills. Explore the region's specialties, such as cheese, honey, and smoked meats, at roadside markets. You may also stop by artisan workshops to see highly trained craftspeople in action. Bucovina's genuineness and peace of mind make it a sanctuary for both nature lovers and culture vultures.

Romania

3. **Tara Oasului:** Nestled in Romania's northwest, Tara Oasului is a region renowned for its distinct cultural history, traditional music, and immaculate scenery. Discover the villages of Negresti-Oas, Certeze, and Satu Mare; you'll discover quaint wooden homes, historic churches, and kind residents willing to share their customs and tales. To fully experience the rich cultural tapestry of the area, go on a trek through the Oas Mountains, stop by the Budesti Codru Moma Ethnographic Museum, or go to a traditional folk festival. If you go off the beaten track in Tara Oasului, you'll find a secret treasure that is just waiting to be discovered. Long after you've gone, the untamed beauty of the mountains, the peace of the countryside, and the friendliness of the people will be with you. Tara Oasului gives a window into a world unspoiled by time, whether you want to go through virgin woods, try the local food, or learn traditional dances.

Romania

Northern Romania's historic communities and landscapes provide a voyage of amazement and discovery, with each hamlet, church, and natural feature telling a tale of history, resiliency, and beauty. You may lose yourself in the enduring appeal of Romania's northern countryside whether you're strolling through the wooden towns of Maramures, taking in the murals in the monasteries of Bucovina, or trekking through the mountains of Tara Oasului.

Romania

Chapter 6: The Danube Delta: Europe's Amazon

Exploring the Tranquil Waterways of the Danube Delta: A Guide to Cruising and Kayaking

The Danube Delta is a preserved natural area that provides a distinct ecosystem of marshes, wetlands, and canals that are home to a wide range of wildlife. Discovering this UNESCO World Heritage Site by sailing or kayaking offers a unique experience that allows visitors

Romania

to fully appreciate the serene beauty of one of Europe's few unspoiled wilderness areas. This is your comprehensive guide on navigating the tranquil Danube Delta rivers:

Cruising

Setting off on a leisurely voyage in the Danube Delta is like exploring a hidden world of winding rivers and serene scenery. Whether traveling by river cruiser or traditional boat, visitors may choose from guided excursions or navigate the maze-like canals, marshes, and lakes with the help of local boatmen. Along the way, pay special attention to rare bird species such as cormorants, herons, and pelicans. You may also get glimpses of otters, wild boar, and the elusive Danube Delta wild horses.

It is utterly pleasant to glide along the tranquil waterways of the Danube Delta. Encircled by luscious vegetation and a mirrored sky, visitors will experience a sense of peace and calm. The ideal symphony of bird noises combined with the calming rhythm of the boat creates a

Romania

magnificent environment that invites guests to unwind and establish a deep connection with nature.

Kayaking

Kayaking offers an unparalleled experience for a more intimate and comprehensive exploration of the Danube Delta. Tourists may rent kayaks from nearby outfitters or sign up for expertly guided kayaking experiences that provide information on the history, wildlife, and ecosystem of the delta. Visitors may get up close and personal with nature as they paddle through little canals and secluded lagoons, passing past ancient willow trees and floating reed beds.

Paddling a kayak through the wild scenery of the Danube Delta offers visitors a feeling of independence and adventure. Every stroke of the paddle forges a stronger bond with the natural world under the vast sky, among serene streams, and beneath the canopy of water lilies.

Romania

As visitors take in the everlasting beauty of the delta, they are left in awe.

Wildlife Watching

The Danube Delta offers unparalleled opportunities for seeing animals, whether on a cruise or in a kayak. It is advised that visitors prepare their cameras in case they see glossy ibises, pygmy cormorants, white-tailed eagles, or other wildlife like European otters and Eurasian beavers. The experience is enhanced with binoculars, which make it possible to identify elusive species concealed among the marshes and reeds.

Meeting the diverse species of the Danube Delta creates amazing memories that last long after the trip is over. Tourists are amazed by the delicate balance of life in this amazing habitat when they see majestic herons taking flight, animated otters playing in the shallows, or graceful pelicans gliding effortlessly over the water.

Romania

Along the serene rivers of the Danube Delta, sailing or kayaking is an adventure full of surprises and revelations, as every bend in the river unveils a new jewel just waiting to be found. Whether traveling in a traditional boat or navigating the canals in a kayak, visitors will be engrossed in the enduring grandeur of one of Europe's most alluring natural wonders.

Birdwatching and Wildlife Spotting Opportunities

The Danube Delta provides extraordinary opportunities to see a wide range of bird species and other critters in their natural habitat, making it a haven for birdwatchers and wildlife enthusiasts. The vast wetlands, marshes, and rivers that make up the delta provide vital habitat for migratory birds, rare species, and native wildlife. This is a guide on wildlife observation and birding in the Danube Delta:

Romania

Birdwatching:

With more than 300 different bird species living there, the Danube Delta is one of Europe's most important birding destinations. The delta's diverse ecosystems support an enormous range of avian species all year long, ranging from beautiful ducks to colorful songbirds and sly raptors. Among the most sought-after species among avian enthusiasts are:

- **Pelicans:** The more common white pelican and the globally fragile Dalmatian pelican each have one last home in the Danube Delta. Take in the stunning birds soaring above or go fishing in the shallow waters of the delta.
- **Herons and Egrets:** Keep an eye out for little egrets, gray herons, and purple herons as they hunt in the marshes and reed beds.

Romania

- **Spoonbills:** As it forages through the shallows in search of food, spot the Eurasian spoonbill, which is distinguished by its spoon-shaped bill.
- **Raptors:** Look for raptors hunting over the marshes and grasslands of the delta, such as peregrine falcons, white-tailed eagles, and marsh harriers.

Wildlife Spotting:

The Danube Delta is home to a wide range of animal species, including fish, amphibians, mammals, and reptiles, in addition to birds. Be alert for:

- **European Otters:** See these gregarious and reticent animals swimming or grazing along the riverbanks of the delta.
- **Wild Boar:** Search the marshy areas and forests of the delta for wild boar that are searching for food.

Romania

- **Eurasian Beavers:** Along the rivers and streams that make up the delta, keep an eye out for signs of beaver activity, such as dams and gnawed tree stumps.
- **Danube Delta Horses:** Come across the half-wild horses, descended from animals brought here by early settlers, that roam the far-off islands and marshes of the delta.
- **European Water Voles:** Along the rivers that traverse the delta, keep an eye out for these little rodents darting among the grasses and reeds.

Observation and Guided tours Platforms:

Consider going on a guided tour with experienced naturalist guides to get the best birding and wildlife viewing experiences. These experts can assist you in identifying different species and provide you with information on the ecology and conservation efforts of the

Romania

delta. Numerous tour companies provide hiking trips, boat rides, and birdwatching tours that may be tailored to suit a range of interests and skill levels. Furthermore, the delta is dotted with bird shelters and observation platforms that have been thoughtfully placed to provide the best possible viewing opportunities for enthusiasts of the natural world.

Encircled by the sights and sounds of nature when standing on a boat's deck, you can't help but be amazed and in awe of the birds you see in their natural habitat and the elusive species you spy amid the marshes and reeds. Every contact with a unique species or an entertaining otter helps one to appreciate the delicate balance of life in the Danube Delta and the need to preserve it for the enjoyment of future generations.

The Danube Delta offers an entirely immersive experience for birdwatching and wildlife spotting, where each sighting and observation

Romania

brings you closer to the natural world and its wonders. The delta's diverse ecosystems and many animals provide boundless opportunities for exploration and adventure in one of Europe's most pristine wilderness areas, regardless of experience level or interest in nature.

Traditional Fishing Villages and Local Cuisine

In addition to being a refuge for wildlife, the Danube Delta is home to charming fishing villages where time appears to stand still. For many years, these native communities have continued to rely on the waterways of the delta for both food and financial support. Investigating these villages provides a window into a world where native cuisine, hospitality, and fishing customs coexist. This is a guide to the Danube Delta's traditional fishing villages and regional cuisine:

Romania

1. **Sulina:** The largest town in the Danube Delta, Sulina serves as the main port that links the delta to the Black Sea. The blend of Greek, Turkish, and Romanian customs in this ancient hamlet is evident in its charming alleyways adorned with vibrant structures. Explore its narrow streets, take in the view of the Black Sea from the lighthouse, and visit the bustling fish market where locals trade their daily haul. Savor delectable dishes of fresh fish in neighborhood eateries, such as fried catfish, grilled carp, and hearty fish soup, which are often accompanied by polenta and pickled veggies.

2. **Sfantu Gheorghe:** A charming community where the river and the sea converge, Sfantu Gheorghe is tucked away at the easternmost point of the delta. This peaceful fishing community is only reachable by boat and offers a peaceful escape from the hectic pace of contemporary life. Discover its marshes, dunes, and sandy beaches—home to a variety of

Romania

wildlife and bird species. Visit the neighborhood fisherman's cooperative to sample freshly smoked fish, a specialty of the area, and learn about traditional fishing techniques. Savor the delectable concoction of locally sourced fish, tomatoes, peppers, and herbs that are known as fisherman's stew. It is often served with crusty bread and wine from the area.

3. **Mila 23:** Nestled deep inside the Danube Delta, Mila 23 is a remote fishing village that can only be reached by boat or ferry. Known for being far from the river's mouth, this remote outpost is a haven for those who love the outdoors and birdwatching. See herons, pelicans, and other bird species while navigating its serene waterways, marshes, and floating reed islands. Visit a nearby fisherman's home to learn about customary fishing methods and have a homemade feast of grilled shrimp, fried fish, and a salad prepared with tomatoes, onions, and cucumbers.

Romania

Experience Traditional Cuisine:
Discovering the Danube Delta's indigenous food is a culinary journey where meals made with simple but delicious ingredients prioritize fresh fish. You'll experience a variety of tastes and aromas that reflect the delta's extensive culinary heritage, whether dining at a restaurant by the beach or sharing a meal with locals. Every dish, which ranges from hearty soups and savory pies to grilled fish and seafood stews, tells a story about tradition, creativity, and the abundant aquatic life of the delta.

Cultural Enthralment : Exploring the old fishing villages of the Danube Delta offers an experience that goes beyond a culinary trip; it's an enthralment into the spirit of the area, shaped by the river's rhythms and natural surroundings. Interact with people, take in their manner of living, and feel their generosity as you engross yourself in the delta's customs,

Romania

traditions, and cuisines. Whether you engage in local customs, learn how to toss a fishing net, or share stories over dinner, you'll get a deeper understanding of the cultural heritage and enduring appeal of this exceptional Romanian gem.

Preservation of Heritage: You will experience a way of life that has persisted for generations while visiting the old fishing villages in the Danube Delta. However, this style of life is confronted with modern issues including economic instability and environmental degradation. Travelers may contribute to sustaining the cultural heritage and scenic beauty of the Danube Delta for many years to come by helping local people, upholding their customs, and promoting sustainable practices.

Immersion in the Danube Delta's ancient fishing villages and regional cuisine offers a fulfilling experience that showcases the area's

Romania

natural beauty, culinary traditions, and cultural heritage. During your journey across the delta, you will discover a world of charm, authenticity, and friendliness that will leave you with lifelong memories, whether you want to view old villages, sample fresh seafood, or socialize with locals.

Romania

Chapter 7: Maramures: Timeless Traditions

Experiencing the Rural Charm and Wooden Churches of Maramures

Cradled in the northern region of Romania, Maramures beckons with its enduring beauty. It is a place where wood-carved churches, ancient traditions, and rural villages weave a fascinating tapestry. Explore this fascinating place to get a glimpse of a world where cultural tradition and rustic charm come together beautifully. Here is a guide to help you visit

Romania

Maramures' wooden churches and rustic beauty:

1. **Traditional Villages:** Wander through the wood-framed homes with their steeply pitched roofs and intricately carved gates to step back in time and experience Maramures' traditional way of life. Explore Breb, Budesti, and Barsana, places where ancient traditions are still practiced and age-old crafts are performed by local artisans. Watch the expertise of artists as they use centuries-old techniques to weave cloth, carve wood, and create ceramics.

2. **Wooden Churches:** Known for its distinctive architecture, fine carvings, and vivid paintings, Maramures has an astounding collection of wooden buildings, many of which are recognized as UNESCO World Heritage Sites. Visit gems such as the Church of the Holy Paraskeva in Desesti, the Church of the Presentation of the Virgin in the Temple in Barsana, and the Church of the Holy

Romania

Archangels Michael and Gabriel in Surdesti. Every church is an homage to the artistry and dedication to the religion of the Maramures. Being surrounded by the scent of pine and the whisper of leaves while standing in front of the wooden cathedrals of Maramures inspires a profound sense of awe for the rich cultural legacy and stunning architecture of this well-known location. Enter to witness interiors adorned with ornate woodwork, vivid paintings, and icons that narrate tales of biblical figures and saints. Every church invites contemplation on the fervor and expertise of the regional craftspeople who created them generations ago.

3. **Rural Traditions:** Take part in traditional activities and vibrant celebrations honoring the region's cultural legacy to fully submerge yourself in the rhythms of rural life in Maramures. Take part in the joy of regional celebrations and weddings, where traditional dances, music, and foods like cozonac (sweet

Romania

bread) and sarmale (cabbage rolls) are abundant. Seize the chance to take part in haymaking, woodcutting, and other traditional crafts programs, or just stroll around the countryside, soaking in the serenity of pastoral vistas and the genuine kindness of the people there.

Preservation of Heritage: Witness a way of life anchored in history and perseverance while facing modern challenges as you take in the rural beauty and wooden churches of Maramures. Tourists contribute significantly to the preservation of Maramures' rich cultural heritage and breathtaking natural surroundings for many years to come by helping local people, upholding their customs, and promoting sustainable development.

Cultural Enthralment : Get up close and personal with a live culture that is as vibrant and enduring as the Maramures' wooden chapels and rustic beauty. Talk to people, take

Romania

in their traditions, and bask in their hospitality to really experience the ageless beauty and cultural diversity of this stunning area of Romania.

Discovering Maramures' ramshackle splendor and wooden cathedrals is an enchanting journey, with each town, church, and interaction revealing a world rich in customs, artistry, and spiritual commitment. You can expect to be transported to a place where time stands still and Maramures' spirit shines brightly, whether you're admiring the exquisite carvings on a wooden church, telling stories to the inhabitants over a home-cooked meal, or just taking in the tranquility of the countryside.

Witnessing Traditional Festivals and Celebrations

Romania has a rich cultural past, with customs centered on festivals and celebrations that are essential to everyday life and narrative. One

Romania

may engage themselves in the captivating weave of Romanian culture via a range of events, ranging from vibrant folk festivals to solemn religious gatherings and seasonal celebrations.

Romanian traditional festivals and celebrations:

1. **Mărțișor:** Commemorating the arrival of spring, Mărțișor is observed on March 1st and involves exchanging little tokens, or mărțișoare. These charm-adorned red and white ribbons represent fertility and good fortune. Bright parades, concerts, and exuberant folk dances are among the festivities that herald the start of a new season.

2. **Easter Celebrations:** Easter is still a big deal in Romanian culture, and it's celebrated with plenty of different customs and rituals. Families get together to celebrate the resurrection of Christ and take pleasure in common blessings, from solemn Holy Week

Romania

processions and church services to joyful Easter egg decorating and sumptuous feasts.

3. **Junii Brasovului:** A traditional spring festival that dates back to the Middle Ages, Junii Brasovului takes place in Braşov, Transylvania. Junii, or young men, wear gaudy costumes and parade around the streets with happiness and song. This age-old, paganism-based tradition symbolizes the rebirth of the natural world and the triumph of light over darkness.

4. **Dragobete:** Romanians celebrate Dragobete, a holiday filled with fertility and love, on February 24. Like Valentine's Day, Dragobete is celebrated with sentimental acts, presents, and customs meant to improve relationships between people and increase marital happiness and prosperity.

5. **Hora:** The Hora is a traditional Romanian dance that is done at festivals, weddings, and

Romania

---

other social gatherings. Hands are linked in a circle as participants enthusiastically synchronize their swaying to traditional music. This fervent dance is a symbol of friendship, unity, and the joyous spirit of Romanian life.

6. **Sânsăvălcea Cerbului:** During the summer solstice, the age-old tradition known as Sânsăvălcea Cerbului, or the "Deer's Jump," takes place in the hamlet of Sânsăvălcea, Maramureș. The mythical story of a deer jumping over a ravine is celebrated with lavish costumes, traditional music, and symbolic rituals, signifying good fortune and prosperity.

7. **Fecioara Maria de la Nicula:** The Nicula Monastery in Transylvania welcomes hundreds of pious people each year for this holy event and pilgrimage. With intense prayers and bright processions, pilgrims swarm to venerate the image of the Virgin Mary in hopes of finding comfort, healing, and divine intervention.

Romania

---

8. **Câmpulung Moldovenesc Hora:** During a vibrant dance festival, the Hora takes center stage in the charming Bucovina town of Câmpulung Moldovenesc. Romanian music and dance have a deep history, and both locals and visitors enjoy traditional dances, folk songs, and cross-cultural friendships.

Take Part in Customary Festivals and Festivities: Immersion in Romania's customary festivals and festivities offers a unique opportunity to explore the nation's cultural mosaic, embracing its diversity and age-old customs. Whether one chooses to participate in spiritual pilgrimages, exuberant dance festivals, or seasonal rituals, every activity reveals the essence of Romania and its people.

Preservation of Heritage: When visitors experience Romania's customary celebrations and festivals, they take on the role of defenders

Romania

of the country's historical culture. Through fostering relationships with local populations, participating in cultural events, and advocating for the preservation of cultural assets, travelers help to preserve Romania's distinctive legacy for future generations.

Romania's traditional festivals and celebrations, from their ancient customs to their modern celebrations, are a testament to the country's perseverance, inventiveness, and resilient spirit. Whether you're looking at the spectacular Junii Brasovului displays, spinning around in the Hora at a festive party, or participating in solemn rituals, every experience is a celebration of Romania's vibrant culture and timeless beauty.

Homestays and Cultural Enthralment Experiences

Homestays provide a special opportunity for travelers looking for a genuine and immersive

Romania

experience in Romania to engage with local communities, participate in customs, and experience the genuine warmth of Romanian hospitality. Romania offers a multitude of opportunities to fully enthrall oneself in its rich cultural tapestry, ranging from humble rural guest houses to lovely homesteads in old towns. This is your comprehensive guide to Romanian homestays and cultural enthralment programs:

1. **Rural Retreats:** Sleep at a typical farmhouse or guest-house tucked away in the breathtaking Romanian countryside to embrace the tranquility of rural life. These rural retreats provide comfortable accommodations in rustic settings, enabling guests to engage in farming, cooking, and handicrafts, among other agricultural pursuits. Get up to the sound of roosters, enjoy home-cooked meals created with ingredients that are sourced locally, and then ride or walk across the verdant countryside.

Romania

2. **Village Sojourns:** Host a local family's home to fully experience the sweet rhythms of rural Romanian living. Village homestays provide a close-up look at traditional customs and daily activities, such as milking cows, baking bread, and tending to large vegetable gardens. Come enjoy friendly meals with your hosts at the kitchen table, where you may eat traditional dishes like cozonac (sweet bread) and sarmale (cabbage rolls) and tell stories long into the night.

3. **Cultural Workshops:** Take part in interactive activities and cultural workshops to learn about Romania's diverse customs and handicrafts. Learn how to weave textiles, embroider intricate motifs, or mold ceramics under the guidance of skilled artisans, and get invaluable insights into the inventiveness and techniques that set Romanian handcraft apart. These intense programs foster the development of new skills while fostering connections with

Romania

regional artisans and the preservation of cultural heritage.

4. **Urban Dwellings:** Stay with a local family in their urban house nestled within one of Romania's vibrant cities to get a taste of the country's modern pulse. City homestays provide guests with an insider's view of modern Romanian life by letting them explore bustling marketplaces, chic cafés, and iconic sites while being supervised by knowledgeable hosts. Explore undiscovered gems off the typical path, indulge in delicious street food from neighborhood vendors, and take in the vivid energy of city life.

5. **Festivals & Celebrations:** Take part in customary festivals and celebrations that showcase Romania's rich history and diversity to go on an exploration throughout the country's cultural tapestry. These events provide a vivid look into Romanian culture, ranging from lively folk music and dance

Romania

festivals to solemn religious pilgrimages and seasonal ceremonies. Take part in colorful parades, breathe in the fragrances of regional cuisine, and enjoy age-old customs that have been cherished for generations.

Advantages of Homestays and Cultural Enthralment : More than just a place to stay, homestays give visitors the invaluable chance to develop close relationships with local people, learn a great deal about Romanian customs and culture, and make lifelong memories that go beyond typical travel experiences. Through lodging with local families, engaging in cultural events, and mingling with artisans, visitors get a thorough understanding of Romania's past, traditions, and principles.

Legacy Preservation: Homestay and cultural enthralment programs are essential means of preserving and extending Romania's cultural heritage by providing local communities with a global platform to share

Romania

their customs and legacies. By supporting homestay accommodations, engaging in cultural seminars, and attending customary celebrations, travelers play a proactive role in preserving and reviving Romania's rich cultural heritage for future generations.

A trip through Romania's heart and soul may be experienced via homestays and cultural enthralment experiences, whether tourists are nestled in the tranquil countryside, fully submerged in a hamlet homestay, or comfortably housed in a bustling city. Every encounter, from communal meals with neighborhood families to practical craft classes, pays homage to Romania's enduring spirit and cultural richness, having a lasting effect on visitors long after they have left.

Romania

Chapter 8: Black Sea Coast: Sun, Sand, and Sea

Relaxing on the Beaches of Mamaia and Constanța

Tucked away along the bucolic Black Sea coast, Mamaia and Constanța entice visitors with their immaculate sandy shores, sparkling blue waters, and lively seaside atmosphere. These seaside retreats have something to offer any tourist, whether they dream of hot days spent sunning on the beach or exciting water sports experiences. This is your guide to relaxing on Mamaia and Constanța's beaches:

Romania

1. **Mamaia Beach:** Known for its long length of golden beaches and bustling promenade along the shore, Mamaia Beach is a favored spot for both swimmers and sun worshippers. This lively location, which is close to the resort town of Mamaia, offers a wide range of services, such as restaurants, beach bars, and water sports rentals. Enjoy a cool drink while lounging on a beach lounger, swim in the glistening waves, or engage in thrilling sports like parasailing and jet skiing.

2. **Constanta Beaches:** The city's coastline is home to some breathtaking beaches, each with a unique charm. Loved for its gentle dunes, shallow seas, and expansive views of the Black Sea, Plaja Moderna is tucked away close to the city center. Mamaia Nord and Mamaia Sat, which are located farther north, entice visitors with their calm atmosphere and provide a peaceful diversion from the busy streets.

Romania

Relaxing on the beaches of Mamaia and Constanța is a tranquil getaway that lets you restore your senses and connect with the natural world. These coastal oases provide many chances for leisure and pleasure, whether you like swimming in the refreshing sea, lounging in the sun, or enjoying exhilarating water sports. Take in the peaceful atmosphere as the sun sets in a blaze of color. The soft sound of the waves and the sea wind will soothe you.

Water Sports and Activities: Mamaia and Constanța provide a variety of water sports and activities that entice thrill-seekers of all ages to come and experience the adventure. On the sparkling waters of the Black Sea, there's something for everyone to enjoy, from calm paddle boarding adventures to exhilarating jet ski rides. Take a parasailing adventure to fly above the waves and enjoy panoramic panoramas of the coastline, or dive under the surface to encounter rich aquatic life.

Romania

Beachfront Dining and Nightlife: Indulge in a gastronomic masterpiece at one of the beachfront restaurants along the coasts of Mamaia and Constanța after a day of beachside celebrations. Savor delicious seafood meals, Mediterranean-inspired cuisine, and traditional Romanian fare, all complemented by eye-catching vistas of the sea and pleasant drinks. The beachfront becomes a hive of nightlife as dusk falls, with clubs, beach bars, and live music venues providing entertainment well into the night.

Fun for the Whole Family: With a plethora of activities to please guests of all ages, Constanța and Maia are ideal playgrounds for families. Make sandcastles on the beach, take leisurely walks along the promenade, or visit neighboring amusement parks and water parks. Families may make priceless memories at Mamaia Beach, which offers a welcoming

Romania

and safe atmosphere with shallow seas and calm waves.

Preservation of Natural Beauty: While you enjoy the beaches of Mamaia and Constanța, spare time to appreciate the coast's natural beauty and rich biological variety. From migrating birds to playful dolphins, these pristine coastal ecosystems are brimming with life. It is crucial to protect these delicate environments so that future generations may appreciate and enjoy them.

Unwinding on the beaches of Mamaia and Constanța invites you to rejuvenate, reconnect with nature, and escape the stresses of everyday life in one of Romania's most alluring coastal getaways. These coastal havens provide a true paradise for any discriminating tourist, whether they are searching for peaceful beachside moments, heart-pounding water sports excursions, or life-changing seaside encounters.

Romania

Water Sports and Recreational Activities in Mamaia and Constanța

Not only are Mamaia and Constanța known for their breathtaking beaches and vibrant coastal atmosphere, but they also offer a wide range of water sports and leisure pursuits that suit both thrill-seekers and relaxation seekers. These coastal locations provide something for everyone, whether you're an adrenaline addict looking for an exciting experience or simply want to relax on the water. The following is a list of water sports and recreational opportunities in Mamaia and Constanța:

1. **Jet skiing:** Take a thrilling jet ski excursion and soar over the stunning Black Sea seas. Take in the breathtaking views of the coastline while experiencing the exhilaration of speeding through the waves as you rent a jet ski from one of the many water sports businesses along

Romania

the shore. Jet skiing is an exhilarating and enjoyable way to explore the ocean and feel the wind in your hair, regardless of skill level.

2. **Parasailing:** Take a parasailing adventure to soar far above the ocean and take in breathtaking aerial views of Constanța and Mamaia. Lean into a parachute-connected harness and launch yourself from a speedboat, gliding into the air while taking in the breathtaking scenery below. Parasailing is an exhilarating sport that offers a unique perspective of the shoreline and a rush of excitement unmatched.

3. **Windsurfing and Kiteboarding:** Take advantage of the wind's intensity and enjoy a holiday where you may ride the waves. Mamaia and Constanța are well-liked spots for kiteboarders and windsurfers due to their expansive beaches and perfect wind conditions. All skill levels of windsurfers and kiteboarders may find excellent conditions at these coastal

Romania

locations, whether you're a beginner learning the basics or an expert looking to get some air.

4. **Stand-Up Paddleboarding (SUP):** Take a stand-up paddleboarding (SUP) excursion to discover the calm Black Sea waters at your own pace. Get a paddleboard rental from a nearby outfitter and ride the board along the coast, taking in the sunshine and the tranquility of the lake. While taking a leisurely walk on the water, SUP is an excellent way to stay healthy, enhance your balance, and establish a connection with the natural world.

5. **Scuba Diving:** Take a scuba diving excursion to explore the Black Sea's underwater environment. Divers of all skill levels may find a variety of dive sites în Mamaia and Constanța, from shallow reefs teeming with marine life to deeper wrecks and tunnels just waiting to be explored. There are dive schools and certified instructors ready to take you on thrilling submerged adventures

Romania

and introduce you to the many Black Sea marine environments.

6. **Boat Tours & Cruises:** Take a leisurely boat ride or sunset cruise to unwind and take in the scenic grandeur of Mamaia and Constanța. Take a tour boat ride down the coast to see expansive vistas of the land, historical landmarks, and breathtaking natural formations. In addition to offering opportunities for swimming, snorkeling, and wildlife observation, many boat tours also let you fully experience the serenity and beauty of the Black Sea.

7. **Fishing Charters:** Take a fishing charter trip în Mamaia or Constanța and throw in your line and reel in the day's catch. Spend a day deep-sea fishing with a knowledgeable crew and a local skipper, pursuing a variety of fish including sharks, sea bass, and mackerel. Fishing charters provide you with all the tools

Romania

and expertise required for an enjoyable and successful Black Sea fishing trip.

8. **Beach Volleyball and Frisbee:** Gather your loved ones for a game of beach volleyball or frisbee on the sandy shores of Constanța and Mamaia for a more relaxed beach experience. There are volleyball courts and open areas for recreational use in many seaside areas, so it's easy to have some friendly competition or just enjoy some sunbathing while being active and having fun.

9. **Beachfront Bars and Cafes:** Take a break and unwind at one of the many beachside bars and cafes that line the Mamaia and Constanța coastlines after a day of water sports and leisure activities. Enjoy refreshing drinks, sample regional wines and beers, and feast on delectable canapés and appetizers while admiring the breathtaking Black Sea vistas. Beachfront eateries are a great place to meet people and take advantage of the vibrant

Romania

nightlife along the coastline because they often have live music, DJs, and other entertainment.

There are several opportunities for fun and excitement on the sea în Mamaia and Constanța, whether you're looking for heart-pounding water sports or lazy seaside days. With activities like windsurfing, scuba diving, jet skiing, and parasailing available, these thrilling beach locations have plenty to offer everyone. So gather your swimsuit, sunscreen, and adventurous attitude, and get ready to make a splash in Constanța and Mamaia!

Exploring Ancient Ruins and Seaside Resorts

Romania's shoreline is a veritable gold mine of contrasts, fusing contemporary luxury with antiquated heritage to create an alluring holiday destination. Discover a plethora of experiences along the Romanian coast, ranging

Romania

from the ruins of ancient civilizations to the lively energy of beachside resorts. This is your guide to discovering Romania's historic sites and coastal towns:

1. **Histria:** Travel back in time to Histria, one of the first Greek colonies in Romania. This ancient city, which was founded in the 7th century BC and is located close to Istria, provides insight into the area's prosperous history as a major commercial center. Take a tour around the remnants of this ancient civilization's city walls, temples, and homes to get fully immersed in its past.

2. **Tomis:** In Constanța, a city rich in myth and history, explore the ancient Tomis ruins. Tomis, which the Greeks founded in the sixth century BC and the Romans subsequently occupied, is most famous for being the location of Ovid's exile. Discover the wonders of this ancient city by exploring the archeological site,

Romania

which includes Roman baths, a theater, and walls.

3. **Callatis:** Explore the historic remains of this important Greek colony on the Black Sea coast by traveling to Mangalia. Callatis, which dates back to the sixth century BC, was a thriving port city that was essential to marine commerce. Discover more about this ancient marine culture by exploring the archeological site, which has ruins of homes, temples, and fortifications.

4. **Beach Resorts:** Take a break and luxuriate at one of Romania's gorgeous beach resorts after learning about the country's rich history. There is a resort location to fit your tastes, whether you like the bustling vibe of Mamaia or the serene ambiance of Eforie Nord. Along the Black Sea coast, unwind on sand beaches, take in the sun, and experience first-rate facilities and friendliness.

Romania

5. **Beach Activities and Water Sports:** Romania's coastal resorts provide a wide range of beach activities and water sports for adventure seekers, from swimming and tanning to sailing and snorkeling. Take a plunge into the glistening blue seas, go on exhilarating adventures in water sports, or just kick back on the coast and watch the waves come in. With many chances for enjoyment and adventure, Romania's stunning coastline will help you make priceless memories.

6. **Spa and Wellness Retreats:** Indulge in a restorative getaway at one of Romania's opulent spas or wellness centers, where you may reenergize and relax in elegance. Savor luxurious spa services, unwind in peaceful settings, and feed your body and spirit with holistic health experiences. After spending time at one of Romania's top wellness resorts, you'll feel rejuvenated and renewed thanks to the relaxing massages and stimulating spa treatments offered.

Romania

7. **Dining and Entertainment:** Indulge in fresh seafood, Mediterranean-inspired meals, and regional specialties at beachside cafés and restaurants that showcase the tastes of Romania's coastal cuisine. Discover the exciting nightlife of coastal resorts after dark, with live music, DJ sets, and cultural events available at pubs, clubs, and entertainment venues along the shore. The Romanian seaside offers a plethora of gastronomic and cultural experiences, whether you want to dine al fresco or dance till morning.

8. **Cultural Excursions:** From your beach resort, take guided excursions and day trips to see the natural beauty and rich cultural legacy of Romania's coastline area. Explore neighboring sights like Constanța's ancient sites and museums or the Danube Delta, a UNESCO World Heritage Site renowned for its varied species and unspoiled surroundings. Take leisurely drives down the coast, pausing

Romania

to take in expansive vistas and discover quaint coastal towns along the route.

Preservation of legacy: As you travel through Romania's historic sites and beach towns, stop to consider how vital it is to preserve the nation's natural and cultural legacy. To guarantee that Romania's coastal riches are accessible and treasured for future generations, support sustainable tourism practices, show respect for ancient monuments and protected areas, and educate yourself about the history and importance of each place.

Discovering Romania's historic sites and coastal towns is a fascinating voyage through time and space, where the charms of the present coexist with the echoes of the past along the stunning Black Sea coast. This enchanted region of Eastern Europe has a world of treasures waiting to be discovered, whether you're gazing at ancient civilizations,

Romania

indulging in beach luxury, or immersing yourself in cultural and gastronomic feasts.

Romania

Chapter 9: Romanian Cuisine and Culinary Experiences

Introduction to Romanian Cuisine and Regional Specialties

Romanian food is a delectable fusion of flavors drawn from its diverse cultural heritage, which includes elements of Mediterranean, Balkan, and Eastern European customs. Romanian food reflects the nation's rich history, abundant agricultural resources, and creative culinary spirit. Dishes range from hearty stews and

Romania

flavorful soups to delicate pastries and delightful desserts. An overview of Romanian cuisine, including some of its regional delicacies, is provided here:

1. **Traditional Ingredients:** The use of fresh, locally sourced meats, vegetables, cereals, and dairy products characterizes Romanian cuisine. The use of staple foods including pig, cow, lamb, potatoes, cabbage, and corn is common, a reflection of Romania's rural culture and agricultural heritage.

2. **Soups and Stews:** Essential to Romanian cooking, soups, and stews provide hearty, nourishing meals under any circumstance. Ciorbă, a traditional Romanian dish made with sour cream, pork, and vegetables, is a popular choice. Add-ons include things like tripe, beef, chicken, or seafood. Another favorite is sarmale, which are cabbage rolls cooked in a thick tomato sauce and stuffed with a flavorful mixture of minced meat, rice, and spices.

Romania

3. **Grilled Meats & Kebabs:** In Romania, grilling is a highly regarded pastime, particularly for barbecue (mici). Mici, often referred to as "mititei," are little grilled sausages made with minced meats (usually lamb, cow, or pig) mixed with seasonings like paprika, thyme, and garlic. They make a great street snack or get-together dinner and are often served with pickles, mustard, and fresh bread.

4. **Polenta and Mamaliga:** Made from boiling cornmeal, polenta, also known as "mămăligă" in Romanian, is a staple that may be a base or a side dish for a variety of savory and sweet toppings. Known for its warming qualities, it's often served with cheese, grilled meats, or stews in Romania.

5. **Regional Specialties:** There are unique culinary customs in every location. Popular dishes in Transylvania include "papanași"

Romania

(fried doughnuts with sour cream and jam) and "ciorbă de perişoare" (meatball soup). "mămăligă cu brânză şi smântână" (polenta topped with sour cream and cheese) and "plăcintă" (savory pastries) staple dishes in Moldova.

6. **Sweets and Pastries:** Honey, almonds, and fruits are just a few of the decadent components used in Romanian sweets. A holiday mainstay is "cozonac," a delicious bread stuffed with poppy or walnut seeds. Fried doughnuts with jam and sour cream, or "papanasi," are a delicious year-round delicacy.

7. **Drinks & Beverages:** Romania offers a selection of drinks, such as brandies, wines, and regional spirits. Famous wines like Fetească Neagră and Fetească Albă are prized for their distinct flavors, while traditional spirits like "ţuică" and "rachiu" are also highly appreciated.

Romania

Exploring Romanian Cuisine: Exploring Romanian cuisine is a delightful journey through a diverse culinary landscape shaped by topography, history, and cultural customs. Every meal in Romania is an opportunity to learn about the many flavors and traditions of this intriguing country, whether you're eating hearty stews in the mountains, sweet treats by the sea, or local specialties in historic towns. So grab a seat at the table, raise a glass of wine, and get ready to indulge in Romanian cuisine. Get used to eating healthfully! (Aim for a healthy diet!)

Dining Etiquette and Must-Try Dishes

Romanian cuisine is more than just delicious dishes; it's also about embracing the rituals and table manners that go along with each meal. Eating in Romania is a delightful experience full of culinary pleasures and cultural insights, from the warmth of greeting to the excitement

Romania

of experiencing new sensations. Here's a guide to Romanian dining customs and must-try foods:

Dining Protocol:

1. **Greet with Respect:** When you go into a home or restaurant, you should say "Bună ziua" (good day) or "Bună seara" (good evening) to the host or server.

2. **Seating Arrangements:** Either wait to be seated or heed the host's instructions. If you're dining in a formal setting, the host could have some seating recommendations.

3. **Table Manners:** Although Romanian dining etiquette is quite informal, it's nevertheless polite to wait to start eating until everyone has been served.

4. **Toast With Care:** It's common to toast at meals, especially when alcoholic beverages are

Romania

involved. Before you take a sip, raise your glass, make eye contact, and say "Noroc!" (Cheers!).

5. **Eating With Respect:** Eat with your lips sealed and in little portions. Slurping soup or eating with your lips open is considered impolite.

6. **Express Appreciation to Your Host:** At the end of the meal, say "Mulțumesc" (Thank you) to your host or server.

Must-Try Recipes:

1. **Sarmale:** Served with sour cream and polenta, sarmale is a classic Romanian dish made of cabbage rolls stuffed with a flavorful mixture of minced meat, rice, and spices.

2. **Mici:** Also referred to as "mititei," these grilled sausages are a well-known street food and barbecue mainstay. Smallies are often consumed with pickles, bread, and mustard.

Romania

They are made with a mixture of minced meats and spices.

3. **Ciorbă de Burtă:** Made with tender pieces of beef tripe simmered in a sour broth with spices and vegetables, this filling soup is a popular comfort food in Romania.

4. **Mămăligă:** Made from boiling cornmeal, this traditional Romanian food may be eaten as a side dish or as a base for a variety of toppings, including stew, cheese, and sour cream.

5. **Papanași:** Fried doughnuts served with sour cream and jam, papanași will satisfy your sweet need. These delicious treats are a traditional treat that is adored across Romania.

6. **Mici cu Cartofi:** Mici combined with boiled or roasted potatoes is a classic Romanian comfort food dish that makes a hearty and delicious dinner.

Romania

7. **Drob de Miel:** This classic Easter dish consists of minced lamb cooked into a flavorful meatloaf and served as a celebratory centerpiece. It is mixed with herbs, eggs, and vegetables.

8. **Plăcintă:** Cooked till golden and crispy, these savory or sweet pastries are stuffed with ingredients like cabbage, pumpkin, or Romanian cheese. Plăcintă is a delicious appetizer or snack.

Exploring Romanian Cuisine: Don't be afraid to try new foods and flavors while you investigate Romanian cuisine. Eating at a fine restaurant, dining on the street, or sharing a meal with a Romanian family—each culinary encounter offers a special opportunity to discover the many flavors and cultural customs of this intriguing country. Thus, savor each dish, raise a glass to a toast, and revel in Romania's culinary delights. Foarte bine! (Bon appétit!)

Romania

Food Tours, Cooking Classes, and Culinary Experiences

Indulging in delicious meals is only one aspect of experiencing Romanian cuisine; another is learning about the traditions and rich culinary history that have shaped the nation's gastronomic landscape. Romania offers an array of experiences that allow visitors to experience, discover, and savor the flavors of this diverse cuisine, ranging from bustling food markets to interactive cooking classes and immersive culinary excursions. This is a list of culinary experiences, cooking classes, and cuisine tours in Romania:

1. **Culinary Tours:** Take a guided culinary tour to experience the many flavors and customs of Romania's towns and cities. Food tours, guided by knowledgeable local experts, provide a special opportunity to sample a variety of dishes, snacks, and drinks from markets, cafés, and street vendors while

Romania

discovering the ingredients, history, and culture that make Romanian cuisine distinctive. Food tours provide a delicious introduction to Romania's culinary gems, from bustling markets in Bucharest to charming villages in Transylvania.

2. **Cooking Classes:** Through practical cooking classes and seminars, master the craft of Romanian cuisine from famous chefs and culinary educators. Cooking classes provide an enjoyable and captivating way to learn about traditional recipes, techniques, and ingredients while creating authentic dishes like cozonac, mici, and sarmale, regardless of expertise level. To get fresh ingredients, many cooking seminars often include trips to nearby farms or markets. This helps participants understand the value of seasonality and quality in Romanian food.

3. **Culinary Workshops:** Take part in cooking classes and tastings that focus on

Romania

certain aspects of Romanian cuisine, such as creating bread, preparing cheese, and tasting wines. These practical sessions, which are guided by regional artisans, producers, and experts, provide a deeper understanding of the components, methods, and customs that make up Romanian culinary heritage. Whether making cheese by hand in Transylvania or drinking wine in Moldovan vineyards, culinary courses provide a glimpse into the creativity and enthusiasm that go into Romanian cuisine and drink.

4. **Farm-to-Table Experiences:** Emphasize the agricultural bounty of Romania's countryside via farm-to-table experiences that foster a connection with the land and the people who cultivate it. Take part in guided tours of farms, orchards, and vineyards with local farmers, producers, and artisans to discover sustainable agricultural practices, harvest seasonal food, and taste fresh, organic products straight from the source.

Romania

Farm-to-table dining offers a special opportunity to enjoy the cuisines of the nation in a picturesque setting while learning about the rural way of life.

5. **Cultural Enthrallment:** Take part in culinary activities outside of the kitchen to fully experience Romanian hospitality and culture. These immersive events allow visitors to interact with locals, exchange stories and laughs, and create lifelong memories over shared meals and experiences. These events range from traditional feasts and festivals to family-style dinners and village gatherings. Participating in cultural enthralment events increases one's awareness of Romanian food, culture, and community, whether one is attending a wedding in Maramureş or taking part in a harvest festival in Bucovina.

Studying Romanian food is an enjoyable and enlightening journey that might include enjoying farm-to-table treats in the

Romania

countryside, taking a culinary tour through bustling markets, or mastering the craft of cooking from scratch. Food lovers have many opportunities to sample, discover, and savor the best of Romania's gastronomic traditions thanks to the country's diverse flavors, rich culinary heritage, and warm hospitality. So prepare to enjoy the flavors of Romania by packing your appetite, rolling up your sleeves, and getting started. Foarte bine! (Bon appétit!)

Romania

Chapter 10: Travel Tips and Resources

Safety Tips

Traveling to Romania may be a fulfilling and enlightening experience, but like with any trip, you must put safety first to make sure you stay safe and healthy. The following safety advice is for visitors to Romania:

1. **Recognize Your Environment:**
Keep an eye on your surroundings and be alert, especially in busy or touristic locations. To avoid pickpocketing events, keep a watchful

Romania

check on your valuables, particularly in public transit, marketplaces, and tourist destinations.

2. **Use Licensed Transportation:** Choose reliable ridesharing services or legal taxis. Verify the fare before getting inside the car, and for extra security and comfort, think about using tracking applications.

3. **Refrain From Wandering Alone at Night:** Although Romania is a safe country overall, it's best to avoid wandering alone after dark in uncharted territory or dimly lit locations. When traveling at night, stay on well-lit roads and in busy areas. Taxis or public transit are also good options.

4. **Remain Informed On Local Safety Concerns:** Make sure you are aware of any current travel warnings and local safety concerns in the places you plan to visit. Keep an eye on regional news outlets, study official travel warnings, and register with your

Romania

embassy or consulate to get aid in case you need it.

5. **Honor Local Laws and Customs:** Become knowledgeable about local laws, traditions, and cultural standards. Respect regional customs, dress modestly while visiting places of worship, and be aware of cultural sensitivities when engaging with residents.

6. **Keep Vital Documents Safe:** Keep your travel papers, passport, and valuables in a secure place, such as a hidden money belt or a hotel safe. For backup, think about keeping different copies of important papers with you.

7. **Use ATMs and Currency Exchange Cautionarily:** Use care while using ATMs and currency exchange services, especially in popular tourist destinations. Utilize ATMs found in banks or other safe areas, and stay away from flashing big sums of cash in public.

Romania

8. **Remain Hydrated and Sun Protected:** With Romania's scorching summers, make sure you drink enough water and use sunscreen. To avoid heat-related diseases, stay hydrated, use sunscreen, and find shade during the hottest parts of the day.

9. **Trust Your Instincts:** If anything makes you feel uneasy or dangerous, pay attention to your gut. When anything seems dangerous, get out of the situation and ask for help from authorities or reliable people.

10. **Emergency Contacts:** Make sure you have the phone numbers of your embassy or consulate, the local police, and ambulance services on hand. Make sure your phone is well charged, and for convenient communication, think about getting a local SIM card.

You can contribute to making sure that your trip to Romania is safe and pleasant by being educated, being cautious, and following your

Romania

gut. Accept new experiences, take in the natural beauty and rich culture of the nation, and travel in comfort and tranquility. Happy travels!

Money-Saving Tips

Romania is formerly a veritably affordable country to visit. You 'll be hard pressed to spend a lot of plutocrats then. You really have to go out of your way to do so. But, if you want some ways to lower your costs, then there are ways to save plutocrats in the country.

- Stay with a Local, Nothing's cheaper than sleeping for free. Couchsurfing connects you with locals who give you not only a free place to stay but who can introduce you to all the great places to see and partake in their bigwig tips and advice. It's a great community to be a part of. Eat lunch out Although the food in Romania is affordable in general, you can save further plutocrats by cooking

Romania

your own feasts and eating your lunches out. A lunch menu in Romania generally consists of three courses(haze, main, cat), and can bring as little as 30 RON.
- Rideshare If you're flexible in your schedule, use the ridesharing service BlaBlaCar to catch lifts with locals between metropolises(or countries). motorists are vindicated and it's impeccably safe(though occasionally lifts don't show up, which is why you need to be flexible). While motorcars might be cheaper, this is further fun and generally briskly. Shop at discount grocers If you 're going to cook or are just grabbing a snack, save plutocrats by shopping at discount supermarkets like Profi, Lidl, and Penny request.
- Hitchhiking in Romania is safe and relatively common. It's not the fastest way to get around but it works if you 're on a budget. Just make sure you have a sign and that you trust your gut when

Romania

accepting lifts. It's a great way to connect with locals while also saving plutocrats.

- Take the train The trains in Romania are slow, but they're the cheapest way to get around.However, take the train, If you 're not in a hurry. There are some night trains around the country as well if you 're going long distances.
- Bring a water bottle The valve water then generally safe so bring an applicable water bottle to save plutocrats and reduce your reliance on single- use plastic.

Health and Medical Information

Ensuring your health and well-being is crucial for a safe and happy vacation to Romania. The following are some medical and health-related things to remember:

Romania

1. **Travel Insurance:** Think about getting travel insurance before your trip that covers unanticipated circumstances, trip cancellations, and medical emergencies. Always have your insurance information with you.

2. **Routine Vaccinations:** Verify that you have had the most recent doses of the measles, mumps, rubella, tetanus, diphtheria, and influenza vaccines. Based on your vacation itinerary, ask your doctor about any extra immunizations you may need.

3. **Hepatitis A and Typhoid Vaccinations:** Take into account receiving a hepatitis A and typhoid vaccination, especially if you want to go to rural regions or eat street food.

4. **Drinking Water:** Although tap water is usually safe in cities, in rural or isolated locations, go with bottled water or a water

Romania

filter. Steer clear of tap water beverages and ice cubes.

5. **Food Safety:** Avoid eating raw or undercooked meats, unpasteurized dairy products, and street food. Instead, wash your hands often and practice proper food hygiene.

6. **Insect Protection:** Use DEET-containing insect repellent, wear protective clothes, and use bed nets to protect yourself from bug bites, particularly in places where mosquito-borne illnesses are common.

7. **Sun Protection:** To avoid sunburn and heat-related diseases, use sunscreen, wear a hat, and sunglasses, and find shade. You should also drink enough water.

8. **Medical Facilities:** Major cities and towns in Romania are home to well-equipped medical facilities. Dial **112** in an emergency. Think

Romania

about bringing necessary prescriptions and a simple first aid kit with you.

9. **Prescription Medication:** Make sure you have enough prescription drugs on hand, along with copies of your prescriptions. For advice on additional drugs or preventative actions, speak with your healthcare professional.

When traveling through Romania, remember to put your health first, keep yourself informed, and seek medical assistance when necessary.

Useful Phrases in Romanian

Necessary to-have Travel Phrases

Experienced travellers who have visited many different nations will tell you that there are several words and expressions that are a necessity for anyone planning a trip. We've compiled a list of some of the more important ones for you, having learned from them.

Romania

You will be far more prepared for your trip than the majority of your movie-loving travelling companions if you are fluent in Romanian and know these essential travel expressions and vocabulary.

1. **Bună ziua / Bună dimineața** - Good day / Good morning
2. **Bună seara** - Good evening
3. **Mulțumesc** - Thank you
4. **Vă rog** - Please
5. **Cu plăcere** - You're welcome
6. **Da** - Yes
7. **Nu** - No
8. **Scuzați-mă** - Excuse me
9. **Unde este...?** - Where is...?
10. **Cât costă?** - How much does it cost?
11. **Meniul, vă rog** - The menu, please
12. **Mai puțin picant, te rog** - Less spicy, please
13. **Apa, vă rog** - Water, please
14. **Pot să plătesc cu cardul?** - Can I pay by card?

Romania

15. **Ajutor!** - Help!
16. **La revedere** - Goodbye
17. **Salut** - Hello
18. **Aveți o zi bună** - Have a good day
19. **Vorbim limba engleză?** - Do you speak English?
20. **Îmi puteți recomanda un restaurant bun?** - Can you recommend a good restaurant?
21. **Există un autobuz de la aeroport în oraș?** - Is there a bus from the airport to the city?
22. **Scuzați-mă, cât e tariful?** - Excuse me, what's the fare?
23. **Aș putea primi o hartă?** - Could I get a map?

Learning these basic phrases will facilitate communication with locals and demonstrate respect for their language and culture. Enjoy your time in Romania!

Romania

Good-To-Have Travel Phrases

Ați putea să îmi faceți o poză vă rog? - Could you take a picture of me please?

Ai unele recomandări? -Do you have any recommendations?)

Ai unele recomandări? - Do you have any recommendations?

Este Wi-Fi gratuit? - Is the Wi-Fi free?

Ways To Improve Communication in a Foreign Country

When you don't speak the same language, communication might still be easy when traveling.

Remember these five pointers while you do so. They are intended to make your trip enjoyable as well as to assist you in communicating with people who do not speak English fluently!

Romania

1. Make sure your English is clear and concise. When speaking with someone who doesn't speak English well, stick to simple verbs, adjectives, and nouns and make your sentences brief. On the other hand, avoid speaking to them in pidgin or in a childlike manner. Use proper language and maintain a natural, uncomplicated tone when speaking.
2. First, follow Rule 1 in your hotel, where most likely the personnel can communicate in some English. Ask them to jot down phrases like "Please take me to the beach," "I would like to go to the airport," or "Where is the closest toilet?" in their own language. You can then provide these written inquiries to cab drivers or anybody else who is ready and able to assist you. When you travel to a foreign nation, one easy action could make your life much easier!
3. Choose wisely who you ask for assistance from. It's time to observe folks

Romania

and consider how they seem! English proficiency is more likely in a younger person who appears to be a student than in the kind but elderly woman grinning at you from a fruit stand. Go into the nearest town to the bank, hospital, pharmacy, or motel if you don't see someone like that. Those establishments typically have some English-speaking employees.

4. If you followed the above guidelines, but the individual you are speaking with only gives you a blank face before saying "thank you" and walking away. It is pointless to wait around, expecting that someone will eventually get the hint and reply; you might even annoy them. Look for another person.

Romania

Useful Apps and Online Resources

Applications:

1. **Google Maps:** Easily navigate Romanian cities, towns, and rural locations. Discover local eateries, sights, and lodging options. You may also get instructions and areas of interest.

2. **TripAdvisor:** Get access to reviews, ratings, and suggestions from users for accommodations, dining options, activities, and attractions in Romania. Take advantage of efficient travel planning with offline access to maps and guides.

3. **XE Currency Converter:** When visiting Romania, quickly compute exchange rates and convert currencies. helpful for shopping, budgeting, and comparing costs across several currencies.

4. **Google Translate:** Convert Romanian menus, signs, and words into the language of

Romania

---

your choice. Make use of the camera function to translate text in real time, which will help with comprehension and conversation.

5. Book lodging in Romania, including hotels, guesthouses, and vacation rentals, using Booking.com or Airbnb. Read reviews left by previous visitors and filter search results according to your tastes.

Web-Based Resources:

Romania Insider: News, events, culture, and travel information in Romania are covered by this English-language news and tourism website. Visit www.romania-insider.com to get tutorials, articles, and helpful advice.

From booking lodgings to seeing the nation and looking for travel inspiration, these apps and internet tools provide helpful information and support for organizing your trip to Romania.

Romania

Chapter 11: Itinerary Suggestions

Outdoor Adventure Itinerary: Exploring the Natural Wonders of Romania

Day 1: Arrival in Bucharest
- After arriving in the energetic capital city of Romania, Bucharest, check into your lodging and take some time to decompress.

Romania

- Explore Bucharest's Old Town in the evening and have a typical Romanian meal at a neighborhood eatery.

Day 2: Hiking in the Carpathian Mountains

- Head to the Carpathian Mountains, an outdoor enthusiast's heaven, early in the morning after leaving Bucharest.
- After reaching your base camp close to Brasov, start your guided trip into the Bucegi Mountains.
- Enjoy the stunning views of the surrounding peaks as you go through picturesque valleys, across alpine meadows, and along glistening streams.
- Come back to Brasov in the evening and spend the night in a comfortable lodge in the mountains.

Day 3: Discovering Transylvania

- Discover the charming cities and villages of Transylvania after breakfast.

Romania

- Explore Bran Castle's fascinating history and see why it is often linked to the Dracula legend.
- Proceed to the UNESCO-listed medieval town of Sighisoara, where you may explore its cobblestone lanes adorned with vibrant homes and important historical sites.
- Take a leisurely drive through the picturesque Transylvanian countryside, pausing to take in the breathtaking vistas and charming little towns.
- Go back to Brasov for an additional restful and revitalizing night.

Day 4: Activities to Get Your Heart Pumping

- Exhilarating outdoor activities are the main focus of today.
- Pick from a variety of adventure activities, such as whitewater rafting, rock climbing, zip-lining, and mountain biking.

Romania

- In the breathtaking natural setting of the Carpathian Mountains, spend the day pushing yourself and enjoying the rush of outdoor exploration.
- Relax with a filling dinner and tell other tourists about your activities in the evening.

Day 5: Danube Delta Exploration

- Leave Brasov and go to the Danube Delta, one of the most biologically varied areas in Europe.
- Take a guided boat trip to the delta to see its intricate rivers, verdant marshes, and abundant animals. Look out for uncommon fauna such as otters and wild boars, and bird species such as pelicans, herons, and cormorants. Savor a delicious seafood supper made with freshly caught local fish.
- Stay the night at an eco-lodge or rustic guesthouse with a view of the delta.

Romania

Day 6: Kayaking and Birdwatching

- Get up early to go kayaking along the tranquil Danube Delta rivers before dawn. As you paddle through little waterways and undiscovered lagoons, you'll be able to fully appreciate this ecosystem's natural splendor.
- Take a moment to appreciate and capture images of the diverse range of birds, including both migratory and resident species.
- Before moving on to your next stop, return to the guesthouse for a leisurely breakfast.

Day 7: Departure

- Take a last walk along the Danube Delta's banks and enjoy a relaxed morning. Leave the delta and make your way to the airport to continue seeing Romania's natural beauties or go on to your next destination.

Romania

This route offers a once-in-a-lifetime journey across the breathtaking scenery of Romania, including the tranquil marshes of the Danube Delta and the untamed highlands of Transylvania. Get ready for an exciting week full of outdoor adventures, cultural explorations, and breathtaking views.

Cultural Enthralment Itinerary: Discovering Romania's Rich Heritage

Day 1: Arrival in Bucharest

- After landing in Romania's capital, Bucharest, check into your lodging.
- Take an afternoon to see historical sites such as Revolution Square, the Romanian Athenaeum, and the Palace of Parliament. Enjoy some local food by dining in a typical Romanian restaurant in the evening.

Romania

Day 2: Cultural Tour of Bucharest

- Start the day with a guided walking tour of the Old Town, which has cobblestone streets, churches that are Orthodox, and secret courtyards.
- To see traditional Romanian architecture and folk art from different locations, visit the Village Museum (Muzeul Satului).
- Discover more about Romania's monarchy and history by seeing the Cotroceni Palace, which was once a royal home.
- Take in a traditional dance or music performance in the evening.

Day 3: Exploring Transylvania

- Set off for Transylvania, known for its folklore, ancient villages, and fortified churches. Discover Sinaia and the stunning royal residence Peleș Castle, which is tucked away in the Carpathian Mountains.

Romania

- Proceed to Brasov and join a guided walking tour to see its historic core, which includes sites like Council Square and the Black Church. Enjoy the food and culture of the area while visiting Brasov.

Day 4: Saxon Villages and Sighişoara
Travel to Sighişoara

- Also known for its ancient fortress and is a UNESCO World Heritage Site.
- Discover the sights of the citadel, including Vlad Dracula's birthplace and the Clock Tower. See the surrounding Saxon villages of Viscri and Biertan to get insight into their rustic way of life and German ancestry. Savor a homemade dinner with a neighborhood family to get a taste of true Romanian hospitality.

Romania

Day 5: Rural Life and Crafts

- Take in the rustic atmosphere of Transylvania.
- Go to a typical Romanian hamlet to discover the arts and crafts of the area, including woodcarving, weaving, and pottery-making.
- Take part in practical workshops with regional artists to learn about their methods and customs.
- Savor a prepared picnic meal with delights in the countryside.

Day 6: Bucovina's Painted Monasteries

- Visit Bucovina to take in the UNESCO World Heritage Sites, which are known for their painted monasteries.
- Visit monasteries known for their colorful murals that portray religious scenes, such as Voronet, Moldovita, and Sucevita.

Romania

- Learn about the history and importance of these architectural marvels from knowledgeable experts.
- Savor local food and spend the night at a classic guesthouse.

Day 7: Departure

- Take some time to think back on your time spent enthralled in Romanian culture this morning. Leave Bucovina and go to the airport for your next destination, or remain longer to see more of Romania's rich history.

This itinerary offers a comprehensive exploration of Romania's cultural mosaic, including the energetic streets of Bucharest, the serene villages of Transylvania, and the revered monasteries of Bucovina. A voyage steeped in history, customs, and gracious hospitality awaits you.

Romania

Family-Friendly Itinerary: Fun and Adventure for All Ages

Day 1: Arrival in Bucharest

- Get to your family-friendly lodging after arriving in Bucharest.
- Explore Herastrau Park in the afternoon. Here, youngsters may play at the playground, ride pedal boats, and visit the Village Museum.
- Enjoy a leisurely evening at a restaurant that welcomes families and serves traditional Romanian cuisine.

Day 2: Exploration of Bucharest

- Begin your day with an interactive tour of dinosaurs, fauna, and ecosystems at the Grigore Antipa National Museum of Natural History.

Romania

- Enjoy a leisurely walk around Cismigiu Gardens, which has a small lake, playgrounds, and paddle boats.
- Explore a variety of plant collections, including outdoor gardens and tropical greenhouses, by visiting the Bucharest Botanical Garden.
- In the evening, take in a family-friendly show at the Bucharest Puppet Theater or the Romanian National Opera.

Day 3: Adventure Park and Animal Sanctuary

- Spend the day with your family enjoying water slides, pools, and water parks at Divertiland Water Park.
- Visit the Targu-Mures Zoo after lunch to get up close and personal with creatures from all around the globe.
- Take a look around Tineretului Park, where youngsters may have fun in the sun and on playgrounds.

Romania

- Come back to Bucharest and unwind at your lodging in the evening.

Day 4: Castle Adventures in Transylvania

- Visit the Peleș Castle in Sinaia, which resembles a castle straight out of a fairy tale.
- Take a tour of Bran Castle, a famous medieval mansion with ties to Dracula.
- Savor lunch at a neighboring eatery that serves regional delicacies and kid-friendly fare.
- Go to Adventure Park in Poiana Brasov to experience obstacle courses, zip-lining, and climbing.
- Spend the evening at your amiable lodging in Brasov.

Day 5: Medieval Adventures

- Take a family-friendly walking tour of Brasov's medieval center.

Romania

- Climb Tampa Mountain by funicular for sweeping vistas.
- Learn about medieval myths and history by visiting Rasnov Citadel.
- Take a horse-drawn carriage trip around the charming alleys of Brasov.
- Unwind at your lodging in the evening.

Day 6: Nature exploration and wildlife encounters

- To see rescued bears in their native environments go to Libearty Bear Sanctuary.
- Take a tour of the streets, turrets, and artisan workshops of Sighisoara Citadel.
- Savor a picnic lunch and engage in outdoor activities while in the countryside.
- Make your way back to Brasov for a farewell meal at a restaurant that welcomes families.

Romania

Day 7: Departure

- Pack and bid Brasov farewell.
- Take with you priceless memories of your fun-for-the-family trip to Romania as you go toward the airport.

Families visiting Romania may look forward to an amazing combination of animal encounters, outdoor activities, and cultural discovery with this program.

Romania

Conclusion

By the time our voyage across Romania's stunning landscapes and rich cultural legacy comes to an end in 2024, we will have a deep respect for this magical country. From the sun-drenched beaches of the Black Sea to the foggy valleys of Transylvania, Romania has unveiled its many treasures to us, offering a unique blend of culture, history, and scenic beauty. Beyond the breathtaking landscape and historic sites, however, is a more profound reality: Romania's greatest asset is its people. We will never forget the kindness, tenacity, and unfailing hospitality with which they greeted us into their homes and hearts. We will always have a particular place in our hearts for Romania, so as we say goodbye to this land of legends and dreams, let us take with us the memories of our travels, the friendships we made, and the stories we shared. May your travels be full of adventure, exploration, and

Romania

Romania's eternal spirit till we cross paths again. La revedere!

Romania

Appendix

Maps of Romania and its major Cities

Romania

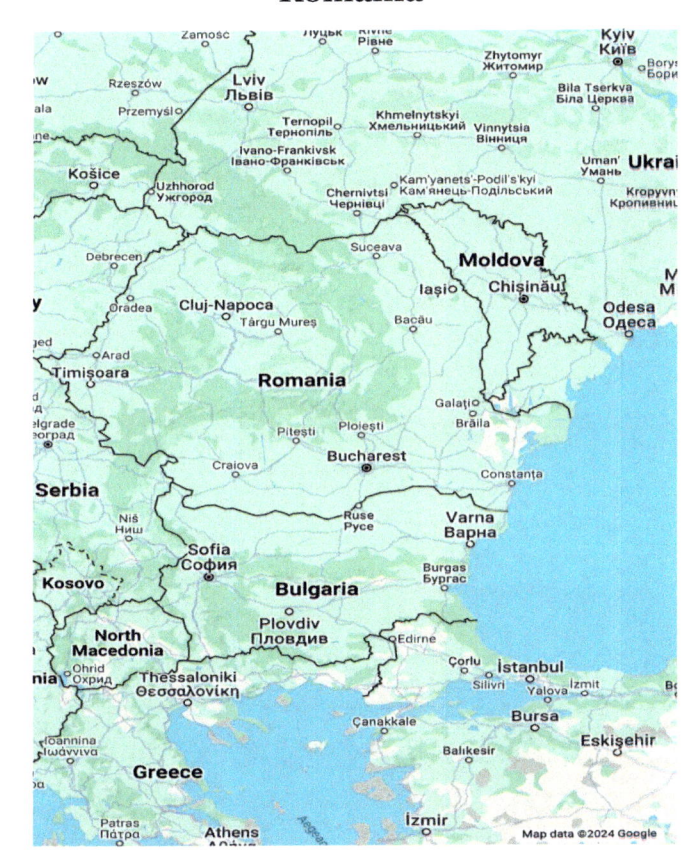

Romania

Transylvania

Romania

Bucharest

Romania

Sibiu

Romania

Cluj

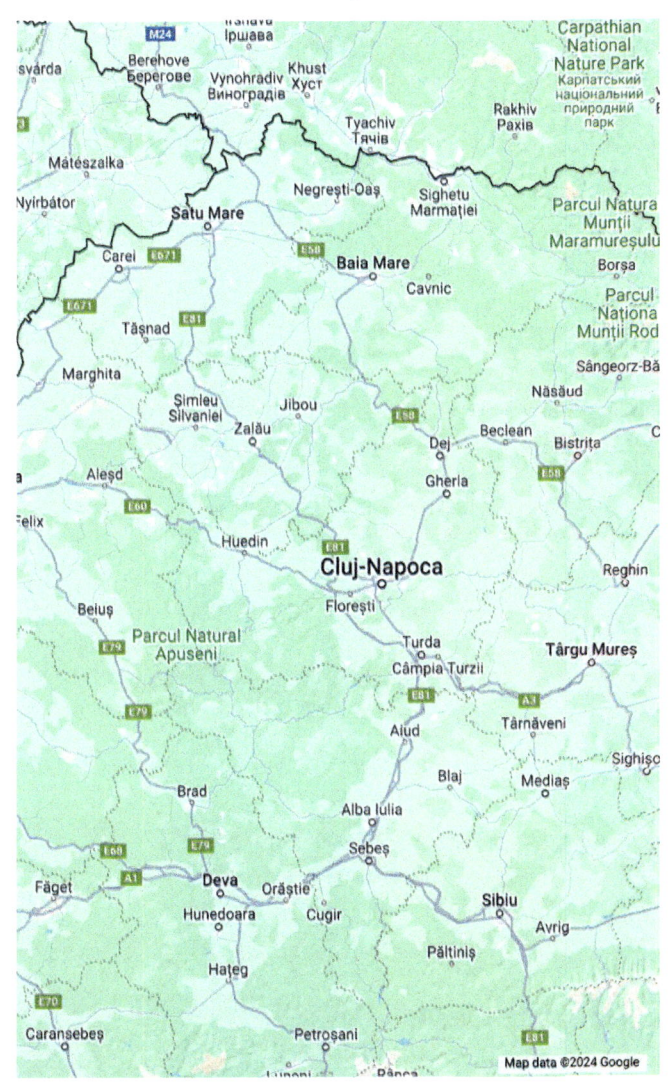

Romania

Constanta

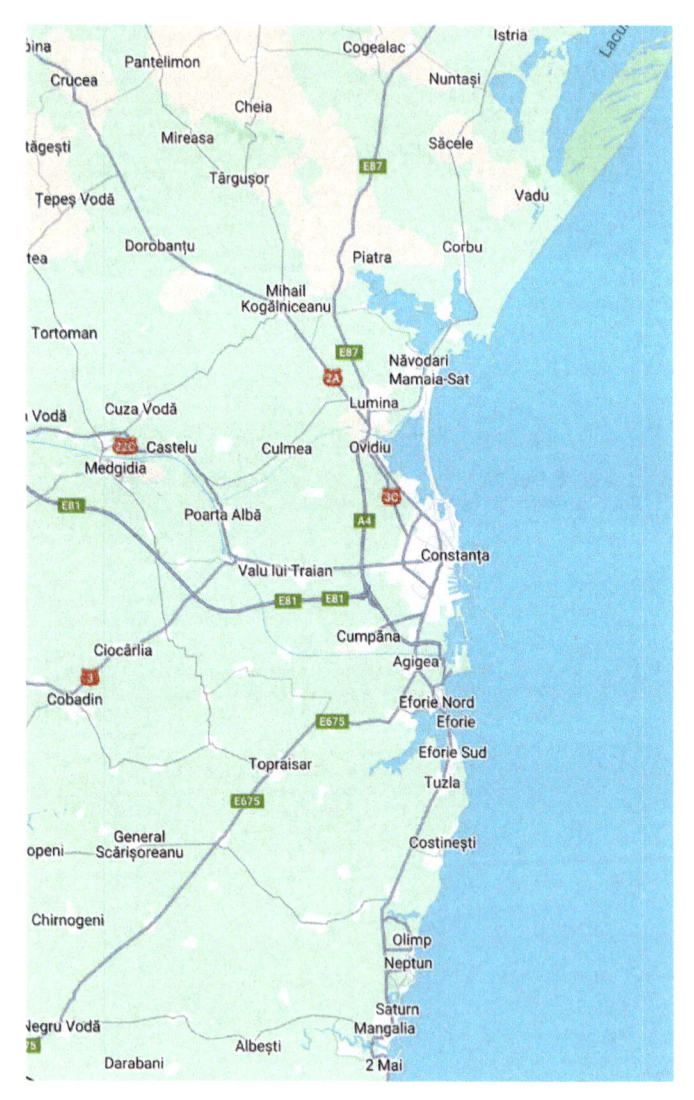

Romania

Brasov

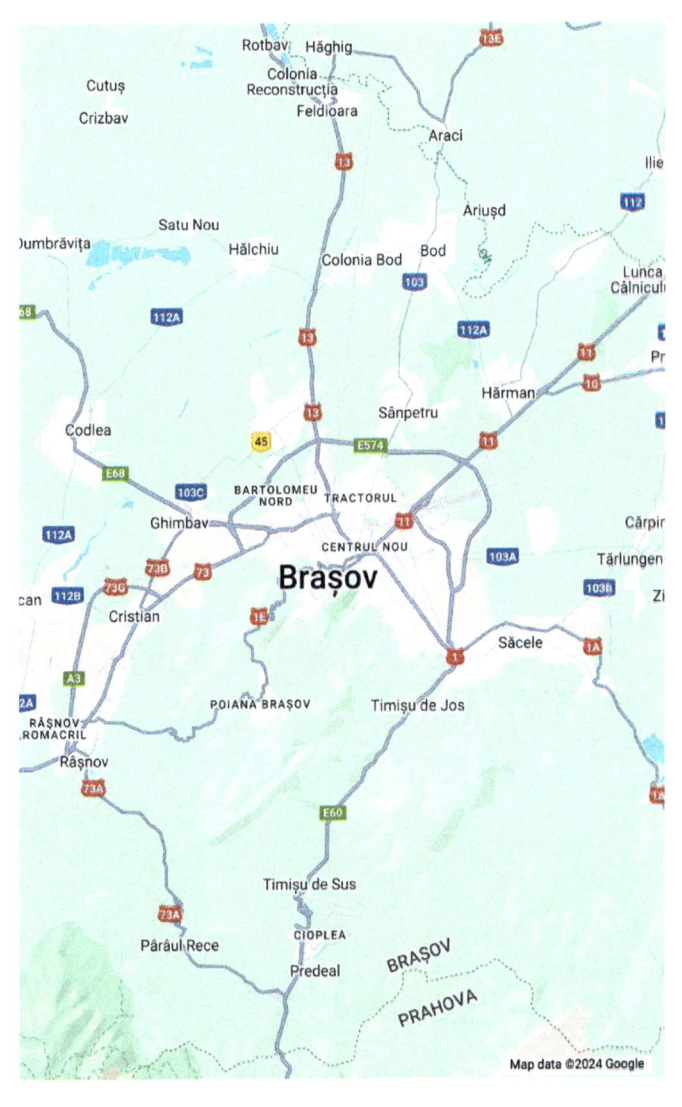

Romania

Sighisoara

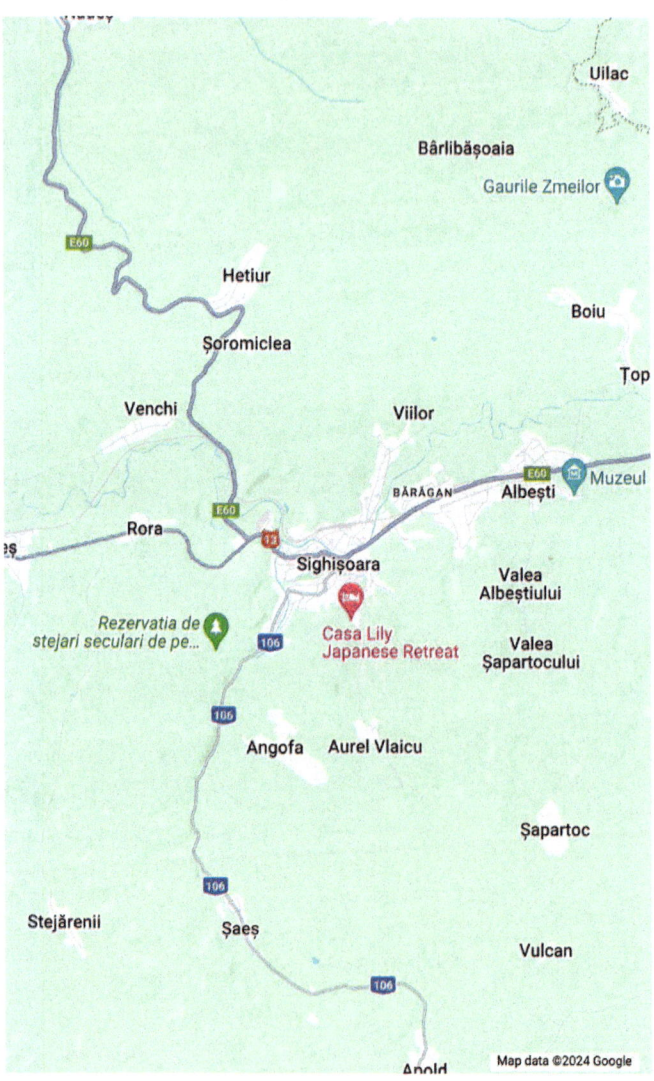

[Romania](#)

Travel Guides by Rose Bordelon

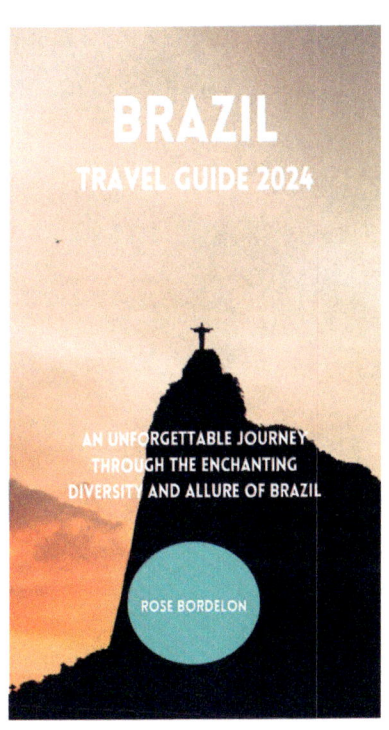

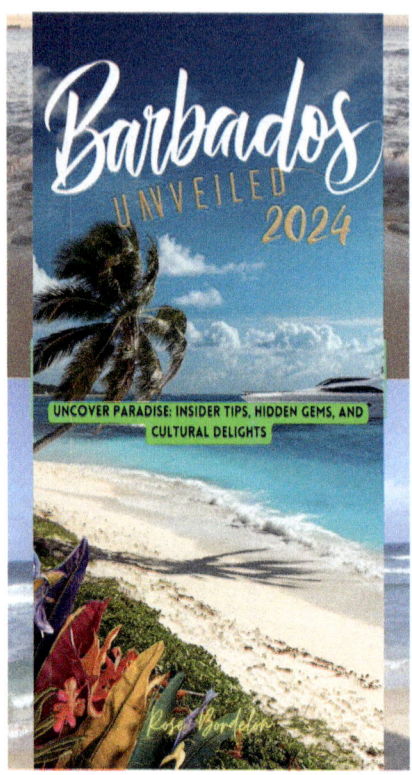

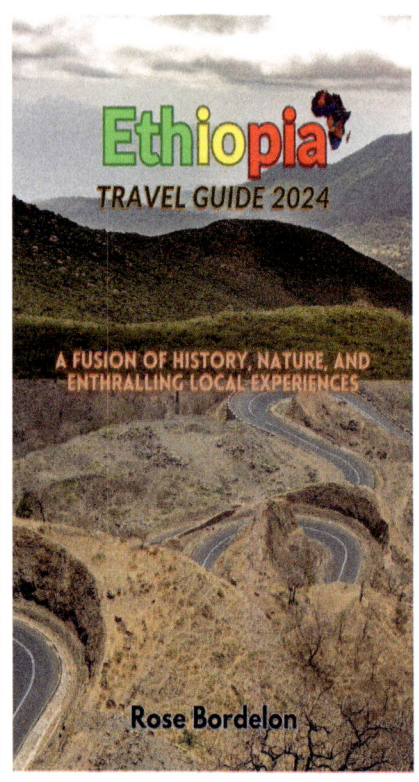

Romania

Printed in Great Britain
by Amazon